THE COLLAPSE OF THE SOMALI STATE: THE IMPACT OF THE COLONIAL LEGACY.

THE COLLAPSE OF THE SOMALI STATE:
THE IMPACT OF THE COLONIAL LEGACY

Abdisalam M. Issa-Salwe

Looh Press | 2022

LOOH PRESS LTD.
Copyright © Abdisalam M. Issa-Salwe 2022
Second Edition, First Print August 2022

All rights reserved. No part of this publication may be reproduced, stored in any retrieval system, or transmitted in any form or by any means, including photocopying, recording, or other electronic or mechanical methods, without the prior written permission of the publisher, except in the case of brief quotations embodied in critical reviews and certain other noncommercial uses permitted by copyright law. For permission and requests, write to the publisher, at the address below.

Xuquuqda oo dhan way dhawran tahay. Buuggan oo dhan ama qayb ka mid ah lama daabacan karo, lamana tarjuman karo la'aanta idan qoran oo laga helo qoraha.

First Edition 1996
"The Collapse of The Somali State: The Impact of the Colonial Legacy"
Haan Publishing,
London, UK.

Daabacaadda Kowaad 1999
"The Collapse of The Somali State: The Impact of the Colonial Legacy"
Haan Publishing,
London, Ingiriiska.

Second Edition 2022
"The Collapse of The Somali State: The Impact of the Colonial Legacy"
Looh Press Ltd.
Leicester, England, UK

Daabacaadda Labaad 2022
"The Collapse of The Somali State: The Impact of the Colonial Legacy"
Looh Press Ltd.
Lester, Ingiriirska, UK

Printed & Distributed by
Looh Press
56 Lethbridge Close
Leicester, LE1 2EB,
England, UK
www.LoohPress.com
admin@LoohPress.com

Printed & bounded by: TJ Books. Cornwall, England.
Waxaa Daabacay:

ISBN: 978-1-912411-46-7 (Paperback)

For my father, my aunt, Farxiya-Foos
Mahamud Osman-Boos, and
the innocent people who perished
in the bloody Somali fratricidal war.

For my Father, my aunt Faxiyo Foos
Mihamed Osman Boos and
the innocent people who perished
in the bloody Somali "nasleed" war

CONTENTS

ABOUT THE TRANSLITERATION OF
THE SOMALI WORDS xiii
ABOUT THE USE OF THE TERMS
SOMALIA AND SOMALILANDS xv
ACKNOWLEDGMENTS xvi
INTRODUCTION 1

Chapter I
THE PEOPLE AND THEIR TRADITIONAL
SOCIAL INSTITUTIONS 7
   Clan Structure and Genealogy 8
   Traditional Authority and The Institution of the Shir
   (Assembly) 11
   The Somali's Traditional Feud Behaviour 14
   The Art of Oral Craft 17

Chapter II
COLONIAL INTRUSION AND THE SOMALI
RESISTANCE 21
   Partition in the Making 22
   THE FIRST ITALIAN COLONIZATION OF BENAADIR .. 28
   The Resistance of the Biyamaal and Wa'daan 29
   Italy's Futile Attempts 31

Reform of Biyamaal and Wa'daan Resistance 32
THE DARAAWIISH RESISTANCE 34
A Brief Background to Sayid Mahamed's Life 36
The Beginning of the Daraawiish Struggle 39
From Movement to State 42
The Battles Between The Daraawiish and The Colonialists 45
The Ilig Treaty 46
Master of Eloquence 48
The Reconstruction of the Daraawiish State 50
The Daraawiish's Diplomatic Victories 52
The Annihilation of the Daraawiish State 53
THE NORTH-EASTERN SOMALILAND SULTANATES 55
Conflict of Interest 57
From Sovereign to Subject:
The Elimination of the North-Eastern Sultanates 59
Preparations for the Invasion 60
The First Casualty: Hobyo 61
The Second Casuality: The Fall of the Majeerteen Sultanate 64

Chapter III
MODERN SOMALI NATIONALISM
(1920-1960) 69
Almost Under One Flag 70
Nationalism in the Italian Somaliland 74
Parties in the Italian Somaliland 75
Parties in British Somaliland 78
The Western Somaliland Political Activities 81
The French Somaliland's Political Activities 84
The Northern Frontier District (NFD) 87
Pan-Somalism 90

Chapter IV
COLONIAL LEGACY 91
The Country 92
Territorial Dispute 93
The Problem of Colonial Boundaries for
Independent Africa 95
THE CIVILIAN GOVERNMENT (1960-1969) 97
Somalia in a State of War 99
The Failure of the Civilian Government 102

Chapter V
THE MILITARY GOVERNMENT
(1969-1991) **107**
    The Rhetoric of Scientific Socialism 109
    Barre's Grip on Power 114
    The MOD Constellation 115
    Superpower Rivalry in the Horn 116
    The Impact of the Cold War on the Horn 117
    Table 1 - The Economy: Major Characteristics of Official
    Accounts and Actual Behaviour in 1977-1983. 119
    Declining Food Production 120

Chapter VI
THE IMPACT OF THE WAR **123**
    Instability in the Ethiopian Political Establishment 123
    The Ethiopian-Somali War 125
    The Aftermath of the Ethiopian-Somali War 126
    The Formation of the Armed Opposition 128
    "The Accursed Days" in the North-Eastern Regions ... 129
    The 1979 Constitution 133
    The Somali-Ethiopian Peace Agreement 134
    Conflict in the North 137
    The Débâcle of the MOD Constellation 138
    The End of Siyaad Barre's Rule 141
    The State's Failure 145
    To a Dead-End 146

Chapter VII
THE DISINTEGRATION **151**
    Power Struggle Within the USC 155
    The Clash of the Opposition Groups 156
    The Djibouti Conference 159
    The Muqdisho Clash 161
    In the Height of the Famine 162
    The Somaliland Republic 164
    The North-Eastern Region (NER) 165
    The Kismaayo Conflict 166
    Barre's Last Bid 171

Chapter VIII
THE UN INVOLVEMENT **173**
    Operation Restore Hope? 174
    The Addis Ababa Peace Conference 176

    UNOSOM's Failure of The Victims of War 180
CONCLUSION **183**
    The Breakdown of the State 183
    On Matters of Leadership 185
    The Siyaad Legacy 187
    The Rise of the Clan Militia 190
    The UN's Attempt to Again Shape Somalia 193
    The State and the OAU 194
    The State's Painful Demise 196
Appendix **199**
    Appendix I 199
    Appendix II 200
    Appendix III 201
    MAPS: Abyssinian Expansion from 1887-1891 207
    Partition of Somali Territory between 1888-1894 208
    Partition of East Africa into Spheres of Influence 1890-91 209
    Secession of Jubbaland 210
    North-Eastern Sultanates 211
    Somali-Populated Territory 212
    Somalia 213
BIBLIOGRAPHY **215**
    Selected Works 215
INDEX **225**

> These people who are raising their voice,
> Who want their land;
> As they struggle for it,
> Oh Allah help them succeed.[1]

Abdilahi Qarshi

—=—

> If I have no escape from tears and impotent anger,
> Why was I created in my mother's womb?
> Why did my mother put me on her lap, carry me on her back?
> Oh God, why did my grandfather and father beget me?[2]

Ibrahim Suleyman "Gadhle"

—=—

---

1. Quoted in Mahamed Osman Omar, *Back to Zero*, 1992, p.85. Somali version:
   Dadkaan dhawaaqaya,
   Dhulkooda doonaya,
   Haddey u dhiidhiyeen,
   Allaahayow u dhiib
2. Quoted in Maryan Cumar Cali and Lidwien Kapteijns, Cry for Independence, *Hal-abuur*, pp.26-29. The Somali version:
   Kol hadday abiid ii yihiin, oohintiyo ciilku
   Uurkii islaantii maxaan, uga abuurmaayay?
   Oofta iyo hooyaday maxay, adhaxda ii saartay?
   Allahayow awoowiyo muxuu, aabe ii dhalayay?

Between the dusk of the day lost
and a vanishing dawn
I am desolate.[3]

Ali Hersi Artan

—=—

I am a Somalian,
And I wonder why
Everything I ever held dear
Is no longer here
And seems to disappear
In fact, it did disappear[4]

Ilwad Jama

—=—

My people have left me
And now I am talking to my soul
To whom will I tell my story?[5]

Abubakar Salim (Abuu Dhere)

—=—

---

3. Somali version (extract from Dalandool):
   Dharaartii duugantiyo,
   Aroor iga daahan baan,
   Dhexdood dalandoolayaa
4. Ilwad Jama, Who am I?, *Hal-abuur*, pp.23-4.
5. Lee V Cassanelli and Bana M S Banafunzi, "A Recent Poetic Lament from Brava", 1993.

ABOUT THE TRANSLITERATION OF THE SOMALI WORDS

In transliterating Somali names and words, I have adopted the Somali orthography in writing Somali names. This orthography uses Latin characters. The letters can generally be pronounced as in English, eg. Marka.

However, there are three consonants which have their own features and phonetics; they are: *c, x* and *dh*. For English readers:
1. *x* is normally pronounced as *h*, e.g. *xeer* read heer.
2. *c* can be ignored, e.g. *Cali* read Ali.
3. *dh* pronounce as *d*, e.g. *dhar* read dar.

   To help the reader identifying places whose names may be spelled differently in early works on Somalia, I have included the familiar older spelling in parentheses, e.g. Burco (Bura-o), Hobyo (Obbia), Baydhabo (Baidoa), Taleex (Taleh).

4. Double vowels are a prolonged version of the single vowel.

ABOUT THE USE OF THE TERMS SOMALIA AND SOMALILANDS

The terms Somalia, Somaliland and Somalilands are all used in the text in different combinations and instances and are not intended to reflect a position on current political boundaries. The contiguous geographical areas of the Horn where Somalis are located are variously referred to as Somalilands — Western Somaliland, British Somaliland, Italian Somaliland, etc., and sometimes using the article (the British Somaliland) — signifying that these are lands where Somalis live.

ACKNOWLEDGMENTS

First and foremost, I am indebted to my wife, Hawa-Deeqa Mahamed Isse "Qihiye" who has been very patient with me during the long days and nights of my writing. I am also deeply indebted to Christina Griffiths who spent much time in helping me to prepare the first manuscript for publishing.

My profound thanks also go to Mahamed Dahir Afrax without whose encouragement, suggestions and help it would have been difficult to write this book. My heart-felt gratitude goes also to Professor I. M. Lewis whose encouragement and advice made my research possible.

My sincere thanks goes also to the following who have assisted me in different ways: Dr Hassan Ali Mire, Abdullahi Salah Osman, Bana M S Banafunzi, Hersi Muse Hersi and Sara Murray.

INTRODUCTION

Like many African nations at the end of the 1980s, Somalia faced economic, social and political problems. Many of these countries were still struggling to survive the upheaval in this period, but Somalia could not solve its problems as a healthy nation. Instead the problems led to its disintegration and dismemberment in a bloody civil war which has claimed more than three hundred thousand dead and wounded, with roughly four fifths of its population displaced. Nearly one fifth of the population fled to Ethiopia, Djibouti and Kenya as refugees. These displaced people have lost their past and their future and that of their children. Subsequently, the country has been divided into fiefdoms ruled by separate armed clans.

After 31 years, the dreams and expectations of freedom from colonial restraint unquestionably vanished; a cloud of human misery and uncertainty spread over the nation as it degenerated into mutually destructive clannish civil war. The political and economic systems collapsed. The human agony is beyond imagination.

As the behaviour of human beings varies according to the type of political order in which they live, the social crisis which was now pervasive created a situation where social norms became void and the individual Somali was left in total disarray, and mental and moral confusion. This sociopolitical chaos weakened and confused moral standards and resulted in the breakdown of Somali state institutions.

What caused this agony and the collapse of civil society? What were the forces which shaped it? Was it part of an inevitable evolutionary process? To what extent did the colonial partition contribute to the calamity? By examining the Somali politico-historical perspective, this book explores the impact of the colonial legacy on the political, social and economic life of the Somali nation, and posits that it is one of the main factors which led to the collapse of the modern Somali state in the early 1990s. It will also briefly consider some immediate post-collapse outcomes.

Although the negative effect of the Somali clan pattern played a major role in weakening the state structure, this book does not attempt to cover its impact and to what extent it contributed to the breakdown of the Somali state.

The first chapter deals with the people and their traditional institutions, and will acquaint the reader, however briefly, with the society of the Somali people.

Before the arrival of colonialism, the Somalis led a decentralised way of life. The colonial powers, however, demanded a way of life contrary to the traditional one. Subsequently, Somalis responded violently to this interference (Chapter II). Accordingly, Somali nationalism is not the result of the influence of western ideology; it sprang from the very nature of Somali culture and was nurtured by a feeling of national consciousness which had existed for many centuries. It was reawakened as a result of external influences such as the establishment of an alien government, the impact of the Second World War and news about the struggles for independence in other countries (Chapter III).[1]

The fourth chapter analyzes the trauma which developed as a result of European colonial occupation at the end of the nineteenth century and the subsequent partition of the territory into five different political entities. The legacy of the colonial partition of the Somali people is one of the root problems of the Horn of Africa. After almost a century, the colonial powers left behind a centralised system of government alien to the Somalis.

For the Somali people the creation of an independent Somali Republic on 1st July 1960 was only the beginning of their struggle for national unity and linked those Somalis formerly ruled by Italian and British colonial powers. It excluded those living in Ethiopia, Kenya, and Djibouti[2] (the latter becoming independent from France only in June 1977).

The preamble of the Constitution of the Somali Republic promulgated in June 1961 stresses that Somalia be a unitary republic with a representative democratic form of government.

---

1. Saadia Touval, *Somali Nationalism*, 1963, pp.83-4.
2. Roland Oliver and Michael Crowder, edit. *The Cambridge Encyclopedia*, 1981, p.250.

However, the democratic parliamentary process which was 'expected' to go well with the traditional political institutions, turned sour.[3] The army took advantage of this situation when it seized power on Thursday, 21 October, 1969 at 3.00 a.m. in a bloodless coup. Hoping that the army had rescued the country from plunging into turmoil, the people could not perceive the real intention of the military junta. But soon a dictatorial form of authority was in the making (Chapter V).

In addition, when people are persecuted and not given a chance to express their grievances, it is natural to look for a mechanism which enables them to do so. The armed resistance groups, which started to form at the end of the 1970s in neighbouring Ethiopia, became the means of expression and they started a trend which was to transform Somalia.

Ethiopia, previously Abyssinia, has always featured large in Somali history. In 1974 a new political horizon was looming for Ethiopia as Emperor Haile Selassie's feudal monarchy was paralysed by a surge of demonstrations organized by the Ethiopian People's Revolutionary Party (EPRP), the Ethiopian Democratic Union (EDU), students, teachers and workers' groups. Emperor Haile Selassie sent his troops to quell the demonstrations. However, this caused more resentment and heralded political instability for the Ethiopian nation. Nevertheless, this new development gave Somalia a chance to pursue its missing territories in a military option.

Chapter VI investigates the impact of the war and its subsequent destabilising effect in the Horn of Africa. The effect of conflict and wars in the Horn became the nail in Somalia's coffin.

---

3. Ibid., p.205.

Chapter VII deals with the disintegration of the Somali state. After the power vacuum created by the downfall of the Siyaad Barre regime in early 1991, the new leadership of so-called "warlords" changed the course of events in Somalia into clan war of a primitive feudal nature. To satisfy their sadism and lust for power, they deliberately destroyed what remained of Somalia.[4] After two decades of dictatorial rule followed by four years of fratricidal war, Somali society has 'lost its bearings as a result of the cumulative erosion and decline of the social, cultural and moral values by which a society lives.'[5] Somalia was being ripped apart as warlords vied for power.

The last chapter (Chapter VIII) deals with the UN's intervention which was intended to alleviate the Somali plight. Because of lack of security, food could not reach the needy as food convoys were being looted and ships were being shelled to turn them away. Relief workers were threatened by armed gangs. The conclusion begins with a critical review of the effect of the colonial legacy on the future Somali state. It analyzes the aftermath of the breakdown of the Somali state and what the future may hold for the Somali nation.

Half a century of colonial weakening of Somali culture, a decade of weak and corrupt civilian government, two decades of repressive centralised state control involving the manipulation of clan mentality, exploitation of traditional rivalry and the collective punishment for any form of dissension, have all created a destructive element in society. All

---

4. Mahamed Osman Omar *The Road to Zero, op. cit.*, pp.205-206.
5. Mahamed Abshir "Waldo", "Somalia: The Need for a New Approach", Nairobi, February 25, 1995.

these have seriously damaged the fabric of Somali nationhood. The subsequent decrease of the political resources of the state, coupled with the crisis arising as a result of the struggle for its lost territory, undermined the state's effectiveness.

While the state's authority was waning, other challenges of sub-national forces of society were growing stronger. The ensuing structural crisis crippled the state's ability to overcome the tide which plunged it to its death.

Chapter I
THE PEOPLE AND THEIR TRADITIONAL SOCIAL INSTITUTIONS

Scattered over a territory covering nearly 600,000 square kilometres in the north-eastern corner of the African continent, the Somali-speaking people form one of the largest single ethnic groups in Africa. With a population of nearly eight million, the Somali people are distributed from the Awash Valley in the north-west, round the periphery of the Ethiopian highlands and along the Gulf of Aden and the Indian Ocean coast to the Tana River in north-eastern Kenya.

The Somali identity and their settlements in this part of the Horn of Africa, generally believed to be what the ancients referred to as the Land of Punt, the country of incense, go back at least 2000 years. There is confusion in determining with precision the origins of the Somali people. The absence of any kind of centralised government led to the impossibility of keeping administrative records or official chronicles.

Somali mythology links the genesis of the people of the area to an ancient communion between people from the Arabian Peninsula, and the Bantu or Oromo people of the hinterland. But the linguistic and ethno-historical advances of the last two decades, with the help of Africa's oral historians, have allowed a more in-depth exploration of the Somali past and have established that ethnically and culturally Somalis belong to the Eastern Cushitic ethnic group.[1] This group also encompasses the Afar (Danakil or Oday Ali), divided between northern Ethiopia and the Republic of Djibouti, the Oromo which forms the largest ethnic group in Ethiopia and which resides partly in northern Kenya, the Saho of northern Ethiopia, the Aweera (Boni or Wa-Boni) of the Lamu coast of Kenya, and the Rendille of northern Kenya.

Clan Structure and Genealogy

The received wisdom on the traditional structure of Somali society traces it through an elaborate genealogy to two brothers, Soomaal, also known as Samaale, and Sab.[2] The followers of Soomaal for the most part led a pastoral-nomadic economic life whilst the followers of Sab exercised an agro-nomadic lifestyle. The Dir, Daarood, Isaaq and Hawiye clan-families[3] are the descendants of Soomaal. Rahanweyn

---

1. Abdirahman Ali Hersi, *The Arab Factor in Somali History*, (Doctoral dissertation, University of California, 1977), pp.21-22.
2. Here Sab doesn't mean the marginalised group.
3. One of the classification used by I M Lewis in *A Pastoral Democracy*, 1961, pp.15-34.

and Digil are descendants of Sab. The majority of the Somali population is constituted from these six groups. Besides these six Somali clan groupings, there are some other smaller communities: (1) the Wa-Gosha who live in the Lower Jubba river region; (2) the Reer Shabeelle who live along the river Shabeelle around Ferfeer, in the Hararghe province of Ethiopia and extending into Somalia; (3) the Shiidle who live mainly in the Upper Shabeelle region; and (4) the Goobwayn who live in the Jubba river area near Luuq (Lugh). These four ethnic groups are of Bantu origin.[4]

There are also the Reer Hamar who live mainly in Muqdisho and Marka. This group is from a mixture of Soomaal and Asian origin and they are divided into Gibil-ad and Gibil-madow. Gibil-ad is made up of the Shaanshiyo, Duruqbo, Gaameedle, Gudmane, Qalin-shube, Sheekhaal Gendershe,[5] Bandhabow, Asharaaf, Haatim, Reer Fiqi and Reer Sheekh clans; whereas the Gibil-madow is formed by Shukureere, Reer Ahmed Nuur and Reer Maanyo.

The Wa-mbalazi or Wa-miini, also called Reer Barawe, live mainly in Barawe (Brava), but also in Marka (Merca) and Muqdisho (Mogadishu). This group speaks a distinct language know as Chi-mblazi or Chi-miini.

As they traded with the Arabian Peninsula, the Persian Gulf, and the East African coastal cities for centuries, the

---

[4]. With these ethnic groups are also found the Mahawey, Wazigua and Shanta Alemod who live in the riverine area.

[5]. Not to be confused with the Sheekhaal Looboge - also known as Martiile Hiraab Hawiye (martiile literally means guest) - who also constitute part of the Soomaal clan groups. Though this group can be found scattered in Somalia, their main settlement is in Jigjiga and Harar in the present Ethiopian.

Reer Hamar and Wa-mbalazi (Reer Barawe) urban settlements are the oldest known in the Somali peninsula. Besides these urban communities, in the southern corner of Somalia are the Bajuun who make their living from fishing, as they live exclusively on the tiny islands of Jula and Jawaya, off the Somali coast near the Kenyan border. This group is of Bantu origin, and they speak the Swahili language.

Marginalised groups are also to be found in the pastoralist society. These are the Tumaal, Midgaan and Yibir. Talented and hardworking, these groups are best known for their skills as craftsmen, though because of this are scorned by the pastoralists.

The Somali people have a strong sense of cultural and linguistic unity. Before independence in 1960, the ecological and economic conditions compelled most Somalis to lead a pastoral life, therefore, they were widely dispersed and lacked the necessary organisation to form a single political unit. This is perhaps one of the main factors that led to the partition of the country into five parts by the European colonial powers.

Because kinship engenders, in a psychological sense, a feeling of closeness to certain people by virtue of being related to them,[6] for the Somalis the clan is the most important political unit in the traditional system. Clan membership is traced through the male line to a common male ancestor from whom the group takes its clan name. Political alliance is therefore determined by agnatic descent and political segmentation resulted from agnatic origin.[7] Descent units

---

6. Eli Sagan, *At The Dawn of Tyranny*: The Origins of Individualism, Political Oppression, and the State, 1986, p.225.
7. I M Lewis, *A Pastoral Democracy, op. cit.*, p.1.

are united by a bond of corporate commitments, the major one of these being that loyalties are to be offered, first and foremost, to ones descent group unit.[8] However, the basic unit of the Rahanweyn and Digil tend to be the mixed-village rather than the descent group.[9]

Traditional political loyalties are reinforced by an informal political-legal contract or *xeer*, by which Somali society settles its disputes. The *xeer* is also the principle defining the extent of the political community. In the words of Lewis, 'Somali contract might be regarded as a form of the social contract of the political philosophers.'[10] Nonetheless, as a way to sanction the defined *xeer*, some form of coercion is applied such as compensatory payment, called *xaal*, for an offence.

Traditional Authority and The Institution of the Shir (Assembly)

As in all kinship systems, Somali political authority was spread through the community as a whole. There was no centre for political control. This reflected the Somali extreme independence and individualism.

Clan leaders dealt with people politically on a face-to-face basis. This traditional authority might also extend over people with whom they did not come into contact, but only if kinship existed between the leaders and the others.

---

8. Mohammed I. Farah, *From Ethnic Response to Clan Identity*, (Doctoral Dissertation at Uppsala University, Uppsala 1993), pp.43-44.
9. I M Lewis, *The Peoples of the Horn of Africa: Somali, Afar and Saho*, new eds. 1994.
10. Ibid., p. 299.

Clan leaders claimed no rights as rulers over their people, in spite of being responsible for all affairs concerning the clan and its relations with other clans. They presided but did not rule over people to whom they were responsible. Lewis reiterates this point in *A Pastoral Democracy*:

> ...even the office of clan-head is generally little more than a nominal title corresponding to the degree of social and territorial exclusiveness which the clan, more than other orders of grouping, possess.[11]

Although the clan-leaders (*Suldaan, Garaad, Ugaas, Malaaq, Imaam, Islaan, Beeldaaje*, etc.) presided over the assembly of elders (*Shir*), they had little executive power as they did not make decisions (*Ugaas ka wuu guddoonshaaye, ma gooyo*).[12]

Egalitarianism is a fundamental social concept in which every man (though not woman) has the right to a say in communal matters. The issue is discussed in the institutionalised *shir* which Lewis defines as:

> the fundamental of government, which has no formal constitution, except that of membership of the lineage concerned, no regular place or time of meeting, and there are no official positions on it.[13] All adult males are elders, and have the right to take part in the *shir*. A decision in the *shir* is reached by consensus,

---

11. I M Lewis, *A Pastoral Democracy*, 1961, pp.36-89.
12. Lidwien Kapteijns, Le Verdic de L'Arbre (Go'aankii Geedka), Ali Moussa Iye, *Hal-abuur*, pp.33-35.
13. Ibid., p.198.

after lengthy discussion and analysis of the matter concerned. This is known as pastoral democracy,[14] though it is a democracy which is patriarchal. The elders are empowered by contractual treaty to direct the policies of their lineage.

The Somali pastoral-nomads have no hierarchical system, unlike their brothers, the agro-nomads. When the clan-head dies, an assembly or *shir* is held to elect another leader.

The colonial concept of democracy was incapable of understanding the centuries old democratic practices and institutions evolved by indigenous people such as the pastoral Somalis.

To ease the running of their administration in the territories, both British and Italian colonial authorities appointed a chief for each clan. The introduction by the British Administration of the Local Authorities Ordinance in British Somaliland in 1950, was opposed by clan leaders, as the system challenged their authority. This practice, also known as the *Aqil* (or *Akhil*) system, caused lineages to contest the office of clan-head. The *Aqil* (holder of the office) was given a salary and some concession by the administrative authority.[15] He helped the District Commissioners in the running of the territory. The same development was taking place in the Italian-administered part of Somaliland. Here the chief (*capo cabila* in Italian) was given a group of armed men to police his clan. The system was intended to create competition among

---

14. Though it can hardly be called democratic as women and other marginalized group are excluded from the meeting.
15. I M Lewis, *A Pastoral Democracy, op. cit.*, pp.196-200

the lineages thereby damaging the integrity of the clan and, with it, the office of the clan leaders. This undermining of the "traditional source of leadership"[16] crippled the future leadership of the modern Somali state and paved the way for the breakdown of state institutions at the end of the 1990s (see below).

The Somali's Traditional Feud Behaviour

Feud is a regular occurrence in pastoral society. Though conflict is a universal phenomenon, the Somali inter-clan conflict is centred on feuds as it aims to injure or eliminate the hostile clan, to seek revenge, to reverse wrongs, and to protect its rights over resources.[17] Because of nomadic continuous movement, a clan may migrate into the territory of a neighbouring clan. Sometimes more than one clan migrate over a given territory, and lineages mix with each other in pastures. These movements which are influenced by the change of seasons from wet to dry and viceversa, create a periodic change in settlement patterns.

During the dry seasons — *jiilaal* (December-March) and *xagaa* (July-September) — which are hard seasons for the pastoralists and their herds, the migrating groups are concentrated at permanent watering places. The rigours of the climate contribute to a state of affairs whereby the greater the competition for scarce resources, the greater the hostility among various clan groups becomes. Ecological tension motivates the pattern of relations between the people

---

16. Ahmed I. Samatar, *Socialist Somalia: Rhetoric and Reality*, 1988, p.49.
17. Quoted in Dolf Zillmann, *Hostility and Aggression*, p.282

even when hostility does not spring immediately from rivalry over common resources.[18]

In the case of conflict within the clan or outside it, elders of a third party or sometimes from the feuding factions meet in the traditional assembly (*shir*) to defuse antagonism. If a member of one clan kills or injures a member of another, the case may (most simply) be settled by the collective paying of the blood-guilt fine (*diyo*) or healing fine (*shafshafo*) to the bereaved or injured lineage.

Traditionally the lineage is answerable for all the external actions of its members, and at the same time it is held liable for their settlement.

The tradition of feuds has acquired norms of retaliation. Once adapted these norms exert a certain degree of control over behaviour related to self-esteem.[19] In the case of balancing reciprocal blood payments, it may be that a deceased's next of kin will take (immediate) action, and tradition encourages this; the brothers, the cousins or the next kin will take revenge into their own hands. Unsettled disputes cause rancour which may be increased by ecological competition.[20]

Every male person in the lineage is identified through his father — *ini hebel* (the son of so-and-so) — and is thereby linked to the line of descent. Through the practice of memorising and reciting the names of one's forefathers, when a man dies he remains in the consciousness of the lineage members because his place in the descent line is fixed.

---

18. I M Lewis, *Pastoral Democracy, op. cit*, p. 243.
19. Dolf Zillmann, *Hostility and Aggression, op. cit*, pp.250-80.
20. Ibid., p 245.

If the cause of the death was a feud killing, this too will live on in the memory of his clan.

The resort to force is the standard procedure expected to be used in case of a feud killing. It is normal to retaliate in these circumstances. The bereaved kin will feel offended and lacking in respect and dignity, so to restore status the relatives have to retaliate. The sooner a reckoning takes place the stronger and more confident the wronged family feels. Sometimes a poet of the lineage might compose a poem which incites his lineage to retaliate for the killed kin and thus regain its status. The victim may become immortalised through the words of the poet.

In the case of external threat, however, (e.g. from another clan) feuding lineages of the same clan will set aside internal antagonism and may unite in common defence.

Many social scientists believe that much of conflict arises out of fear of imagined threats, and that the stuff of social conflict is misunderstanding. A situation may develop into what social scientists call autistic hostility, that is when people, lacking information about others fail to understand the reasoning behind the others' actions. The rival groups thus commit atrocities and justify their actions based on wrong premises. Worse, both rival sides come to see themselves as well-intentioned and in the right, and their enemy as mistaken and threatening. This may help to explain the horror which followed in the wake of the fall of Siyaad Barre in January 1991 and the subsequent failure and collapse of the Somali state.

It may seem that the Somalis are naturally aggressive and have a bellicose culture. But wide ranging studies of social behaviour find that aggressiveness occurs with such regularity and persistence to suggest that it is part of human nature. The course of human behaviour over the centuries, across cultures, or during early periods of child development almost always has included aggression.[21] Nevertheless, although human beings may be born with biological predispositions towards aggression, social learning appears to be more important in determining when and where aggression takes place. Whether aggression occurs depends on the social and physical environment.[22] How and to what extent it is exhibited depends much more on social learning, thus, by becoming tolerant of warlike behaviour, society comes to approve of or encourage a social pattern which in the end promotes and motivates further conflict. It is worth mentioning that history tells of cultures long hostile but which can then experience centuries of harmony, an example is that of the Japanese which had centuries of historical feuds.

The Art of Oral Craft

Somali society — especially the pastoral — is portrayed as a naturally aggressive one. This view is refuted by the evidence presented by Somali oral culture. Art is believed, by some, to be the reflection of people's tradition which develops according to their environment.[23]

The significance which the Somalis place on the oral arts is one of the most extraordinary features in their cultural and political life. They especially value oral verse as the "intimate

---

21. Ibid., p. 280.
22. Kenneth J Gergen & Mary J Gergen, *Social Psychology*, 1981 pp.278-79
23. Mahamed D. Afrax, "The Mirror of Culture," in *The Somali Challenge*, ed. Ahmed I. Samatar, 1994, pp. 233-249.

workings of people's lives"[24] and cultivate poetry extensively. These characteristics have been noted by all Somali scholars and those who have visited the Somalilands. Somalis are often described as a "nation of bards",[25] as for them "language and culture take precedence over material [wealth]".[26] For them, poetry is a means of mass communication and a mechanism to present their case persuasively.

Living in a demanding environment of continuous mobility and danger, the Somali nomads interpret life's different faces through lyric verses.[27] Thus, the poet is considered the public relations officer of the clan and its spokesperson. One can defend one's property or rights not only by force but also with words. When an individual or a group has a case against another individual or group, the case might be taken to the elders and it ends with an assembly (*shir*) where it is discussed. All males are entitled to take part in the gathering, where they can give their opinion. The art of the oral dominates the meeting, with the orator (*codkar*) and the poet (*gabayaa*) as the principal speakers. The law suit or case (*gar*) is put before the council of experts in traditional law (*xeerbeegti*) which is composed, like any modern court of law, of a chairman (*gudoomiye*), word-bearer (*doodqaade*) and witnesses (*marqaatiyaal*). Each individual or group is asked if he or they claim/defend for themselves or select someone to claim/defend for them. Judges

---

24. Said S. Samatar, *Oral Poetry and Somali Nationalism*, 1982, pp. 2-50.

25. Burton, Isabel; ed., *First Footsteps in East Africa by Captain Sir Richard F. Burton*, 1894, Vol.I. p.15.

26. Abdi Sheikh-Abdi, *Divine Madness*, 1992, p.23.

27. Said S. Samatar, *Oral Poetry and Somali Nationalism*, op. cit., pp.34-40.

are selected according to their reputation. Being a judge is one of the most respected roles one can have. It is a role vested with honour as evidenced by Ini Sanweyne who is famous all over the country for his righteous judgement. A judge has to arbitrate according to the truth (*xaq*). If he shows any partiality, he is dishonoured and loses dignity and consequently falls into a status of "he whose daughter would not be married" (*gabadhaa guurwaa*).[1]

The plaintiff(s) and the defendant(s) most often present their case in an articulate manner expounding in traditional history and proverbs, recounting similar cases, sometimes in poetry. They are a match for any modern court where the speaker must be able to defend his case.

The performance of the speaker is judged by his knowledge of customary law, his memory, his response to the argument of his adversary and his ability to convince the court of the merits of his case.[2] The respect which is paid to the orator is based on his capacity as speaker and not as his ability as a fighter.

The spoken word for Somalis is more powerful than arms. A poor defendant is one who lacks oratorical prowess (*af-garooc*), and also one who cannot defend himself or his property. After a prolonged and sometimes heated debate the judges decide the case. They scrutinise the matter presented to them as best they can. The authority and power of the *xeerbeegti* (judges) come from the consensus that their judgement would be impartial.[3]

---

1. Ibid., p.33.
2. Ibid., p.32.
3. Ibid., p.35.

There is a story which tells of a man whose son lost a case. When he asked if his son had accepted the verdict, he was told "yes, he accepted with apologies". The father then remarked: "He is my rightful son and I am proud of him", underlining that by accepting defeat in the traditional court, his son had acted properly. Alternatively, he could have been *gar-maqaate* (one who refuses judgement). The unreasonable individual is seen as a coward (*fulay*), one of the worst attributes of man, and is viewed as one who fears righteousness. To refuse a verdict is tantamount to challenging the wisdom of the judges and the traditional institutions of persuasion and reasoning in front of God (*gar diid waa Alla diid*).

Chapter II

COLONIAL INTRUSION AND THE SOMALI RESISTANCE

European exploration opened the door to colonialism. Among the first European explorers who reached the Somaliland coast were the Englishman William Christopher who reached the Geledi Sultanate in 1843 and Captain Charles J. Cruttenden who penetrated the interior land in the north-east.[4] During the same period the French Commodore Charles Guillain explored the southern coast, Richard F. Burton reached Zeyla (Zeila) and Berbera in the 1850s, John Speke, a protégé of Burton, started out from Las Qorey (Las Khorai), in the north-eastern part of Somaliland, and reached up to Nugaal in central Somaliland. The Frenchman Georges

---

4. Robert L Hess, *Italian Colonialism in Somalia*, 1966, pp.9-11.

Révoil penetrated the Dharoor Valley (Daror), Count Porro, unfortunately, was killed in Western Somaliland in 1885, and F.L. James, more fortunate than Count Porro, reached Western Somaliland in the same period.[5] However, it was the German explorer, Carl von der Decken, who travelled most extensively in the interior of Somaliland, from 1859 until his death in Bardheere (Bardera) in 1865.[6]

The opening of the Suez Canal in 1869 created a geopolitical situation which increased the competition for control of the coast along the Red Sea and the Indian Ocean among the European colonial powers.[7] This colonial competition had a devastating effect on the centuries-old independence of the Somalis. The ambition to control the coast as well the interior was not only that of the British, other colonial powers namely France, Italy Germany, and Abyssinia (former name of present Ethiopia) had the same objectives.

Partition in the Making

Britain settled in Aden in 1839 using it as a supply station for the route to the Far East. She took interest in the Somali coast because of its provision of fresh meat and vegetables for her Aden garrison.

In the early 1860s, the Khedive Ismail of Egypt, in the name of the Pasha of Turkey and the Sublime Porte, began to establish his sovereignty over the ports of the Red Sea by appointing an Egyptian governor for the whole coast from Suez to Cape Guardafui. In 1875 the Egyptians took

---

5. Ibid., pp.31-32.
6. Ibid, p.11.
7. Saadia Touval, *Somali Nationalism, op. cit.*, p.3.

possession of Zeyla, marched inland and occupied Harar where they set up an administration which was to last ten years.[8]

The Khedive claimed dominion over the whole Somali coast and dispatched a naval expedition to the mouth of the Jubba river to link the southern Sudan and the Great Lakes with East Africa. Egyptian troops were landed at Kismaayo but they were withdrawn following a protest from Britain, on behalf of the Sultan of Zanzibar, who also claimed this part of the coast.[9] Britain's objection to the Turkish and Egyptian claim was settled with an agreement signed in September 1877 recognising Egyptian jurisdiction over the Somaliland coast.[10]

Following the successful uprising in the Sudan by the Mahdist Movement in 1885, Egypt had to withdraw its forces from the Somaliland coast and the route to Harar, to reinforce its control in the Sudan.

To stop its European rivals from filling the gap left by the Egyptian withdrawal, the British government signed treaties with the Somali clans living along the Red Sea. This was to become British Somaliland.

In 1886, Britain and Germany, who were both competing for 'spheres of influence' in East Africa, agreed to recognise the sovereignty of the Sultan of Zanzibar over parts of the East African coast to a depth of ten miles, including certain ports as far as Warsheikh.[11] The vagueness of the 1886 Anglo-German

---

8. Somali Republic, *The Somali Peninsula: A New Light on Imperial Motives*, 1962, pp.19-20.
9. Ibid., pp.19-20.
10. Ibid., p.34
11. Ibid., pp.1-5.

Agreement gave Germany a chance to secure possession of the great lakes, for not only was the country north of the River Tana left free to German enterprise, so was the country to the northwest of the British sphere. The matter was settled in 1890 when Germany, in consideration for Britain's secession of Heligoland, withdrew her protectorate over the adjoining coast up to Kismaayo (Kismayu), and surrendered her claims to territories north of the Tana.[12] Thus a vast area, reaching to the western watershed of the Nile,[13] fell into the British sphere of influence, an influence then exerted by the Imperial British East Africa Company. This company was formed primarily as a trading venture, but by Royal Charter in 1888, it was charged with the administration of this area. Following Germany's withdrawal, therefore, the Company, by agreement with the Sultan of Zanzibar, assumed responsibility, in 1891, for the administration of Jubbaland.[14]

What began, then, as a trading venture in Jubbaland ended in a colonial administration, and the Company was vested with political and administrative functions that were beyond its capacity.[15] In 1895 A.H. Hardinge of the British Foreign Office visited the 'Province' and proclaimed the establishment of British colonial rule.

From this period Britain created another area out of the Jubbaland, a territory which was later to be known as the Northern Frontier District (NFD).

---

12. Ibid., pp.1-5.
13. Moyse-Barlett, H.; *The History of the King's African Rifles*, 1956, p.54.
14. Ibid., pp.1-5.
15. Ibid., p.7.

Until the nineteenth century Abyssinians were limited to the central highlands of Ethiopia. A few years before the accession to power of Menelik II (King of Shoa) as Emperor in 1889, they started to expand their power beyond the Amhara Highlands.[16] Menelik took advantage of the rivalry between European powers. Under a treaty of alliance between Italy and Shoa, Italy in September 1890 secured Christian Abyssinia's accession to the Brussels General Act of 1890 which intended to protect 'the aboriginal populations of Africa'. However, in Menelik's case his accession to the Brussels General Act merely legalized the import of firearms, and thus enabled him to realise his imperial plans.[17]

Harar had been built, for the greater part, in the sixteenth century, and had soon become the richest town in East Africa, an independent city state, and a centre of commerce and of Islamic learning.[18] It was the greatest prize that Menelik could win, for not only was Harar and the neighbouring highland rich and fertile, it was a mountain stronghold that protected the Somali lowlands from Abyssinian penetration and vice versa.

In 1886 Menelik sent an army against Harar under Ras Waldo Gabriel but it was defeated by Emir Abdullahi. Then in February 1887, Menelik himself with an army of 30,000 met the Hararis (or Adaris, as the Harar people are also known)

---

16. Ibid., p.47.
17. Somali Republic, *The Somali Peninsula: A New Light on Imperial Motives*, 1962, pp.34-35.
18. J.S. Trimingham, *Islam in Ethiopia*, 1952, pp.140-150.

at Ghalauko and speedily routed them in a battle.[19] From taking control of the city state of Harar, in 1887, Menelik's marauding troops next target was to be the Somalis[20] in what was developing as the Western Somaliland.

The need for a refuelling station on the Red Sea to strengthen their naval communication with their Indo-China and Madagascar dominions, led France to gain access to Obok, on the extreme north-west edge of Somaliland territory, establishing a formal French colony and protectorate in 1885, which was to become known as French Somaliland.

Following an agreement between France and Britain in 1888, the two countries recognized each other's claims to a 'Protectorate' on the west and east side respectively of the Zeyla to Harar caravan route. This was bound to conflict with Italy's interpretation of the Treaty of Uccialli with Abyssinia. By this treaty Italy acquired, in her view, a protectorate over the whole of Abyssinia. Britain acceded to this view but France contested, and Menelik, for the time being, ignored it.[21]

Menelik's interpretation of the Uccialli Treaty resulted in antagonising Italy, and his relations with France became more cordial. By a concession in 1894 and again in 1896 he permitted the French to construct a railway connecting Abyssinia with Djibouti.[22] On March 1896, tension between Abyssinia and Italy culminated in a confrontation between the

---

19. Somali Republic, *The Somali Peninsula: A New Light on Imperial Motives*, 1962, pp.28-29.
20. Ibid., p.53.
21. Ibid., pp.32-3.
22. Ibid., p.44.

two armies at Adowa where the Italians were overwhelmed and outmanoeuvred, resulting in a complete victory for Menelik.

A Peace Treaty was signed in the autumn of 1896 in which Italy renounced the Treaty of Uccialli and recognised the full sovereignty and independence of Abyssinia.[23]

The Italian defeat at Adowa was a 'decisive event in the history of the Horn of Africa because it appears to have forced the three European powers to a recognition of Menelik's independence which made it desirable for them to secure from Menelik recognition of their colonial boundaries, without much thought to Menelik's own colonial ambitions'.[24]

Italy, delayed by its internal problems, entered late to 'the African feast as a poor relation'.[25] They created a colony in the Benaadir (Benadir) in the south, which was under the suzerainty of the Sultan of Zanzibar.[26] Italy was concerned about the interest shown by the British and Germans in the north-east part of Somaliland where there were two antagonistic sultanates: the Majeerteen Sultanate of Boqor Osman and the Hobyo (Obbia) Sultanate of Sultan Yusuf Ali Kenadid.[27] These Sultanates of Majeerteen and Hobyo had developed diverse and very effective political organization with measures of centralized authority over relatively large territories.

---

23. Ibid., pp.44-45.
24. Ibid., p.45.
25. A H M Jones et Elizabeth Monroe, *A History of Abyssinia*, 1937, pp136-7
26. Said S. Samatar and David D. Laitan, *Somalia: Nation in Search of a State, op. cit.*, p.51.
27. Saadia Touval, *Somali Nationalism, op. cit.*, pp.41-45.

To avert the influence of its colonial antagonists, Italy concluded a treaty of protectorate with the Sultanate of Hobyo on 8 February 1889 and, after long resistance, with Boqor Osman on 7 April of the same year.[28] This new deal prompted Germany to object to the treaties, claiming that she had priority over Italy in the area. The case was taken to Berlin, and after having considered Article 34 of the General Act of the Berlin Conference of 1884, the court ruled in favour of Italy.[29]

The partition of Somaliland was already developing during this period. So, too, was an organised form of Somali resistance. The fate of the Somalis would be decided by the outcome of this resistance.

THE FIRST ITALIAN COLONIZATION OF BENAADIR

The first Italian interest in the Somali peninsula and East Africa dates back to 1885, when captain Antonio Cecchi was sent on a mission to explore an outlet for Italian emigration along the coast of south Somaliland. Behind this initial interest was the then Italian Foreign Minister, Pasquale Mancini, whose ambition and plans envisaged extending Italian possession beyond Eritrea, which Italy had taken in February 1885.

On 12 August 1892 Italy received in lease the Benaadir coast from the Sultan of Zanzibar, adding to its successful conclusion in 1888 and 1889 protectorate agreements with the north-eastern sultanates of Majeerteen and Hobyo.

---

28. Robert L Hess, *Italian Colonialism in Somalia*, 1966, pp.24-28.
29. Ibid., p.27.

Instead of adopting a system of crown colony like in Eritrea, Italy preferred to form a system of indirect rule where the "institution of salaried chiefs in each clan were the point of contact between the government and its colonial subjects".[30]

The running of the colony, therefore, was given to the Filonardi Company (Societá Filonardi). It was given the right to exploit and the responsibility to oversee security.

By adapting the policy of capitalising on other people's possession it was natural that Italy should meet with some resistance. Ironically, neither the Italian government nor Filonardi had forseen such circumstances.

The Resistance of the Biyamaal and Wa'daan

Everything seemed quiet for Vincenzo Filonardi, the administrator of the Societá Filonardi, when he disembarked at Marka in October 1893 to take possession of the colony. But during this visit, Lieutenant Maurizio Talamone, the captain of one of the ships, was stabbed to death.[31]

The incident was the first sign of opposition to Italian intrusion in the southern part of Somaliland. Centred mainly around Marka, the resistance, led by the Biyamaal clan, penetrated further to the north near Muqdisho and into the interior reaching the area of the Wa'daan clan who also formed a resistance against the intruders. The Biyamaal clan, which is the largest and most powerful of the Dir clan-family

---

30. Virginia Luling, *The Social Structure of Southern Somali Tribes*, 1971, p.213.
31. Hassan Osman Ahmed, "La Cittá di Marka, I Biimaal e il Dominio sulla Costa Somala, pp.78-80.

in the southern Somaliland, live in the area behind the coast from Marka to Jamaame, beside the river Shabeelle.[32] While the Biyamaal resistance front stretched along the Shabeelle River south from Marka, the Wa'daan clans fought in the area south from the powerful Geledi sultanate in Afgooye, on the Shabeelle river.

Following the Talamone stabbing incident, many Marka elders were arrested and deported to Eritrea, and the town and its surroundings were bombarded. In a counter-attack, the Biyamaal and Wa'daan began to siege the town, and blocked communications with the interior.[33] Blockading Marka meant ruin for the population of the town and that of the people who lived in its suburbs, as the port city depended on trading with the hinterland. The people of Marka could not survive without the agricultural commodities of the Shabeelle River area and the pastoral products of the interior. To meet the town's food requirement, the Filonardi Company had to supply the population by ship.

The conflict caught the Filonardi Company by surprise, and to meet the conditions it was necessary to increase its military prowess. What they believed would have been an effortless acquisition was turning into a sour and complicated operation.

The crisis prompted Filonardi to ask his government for financial and military help. However, the Italian government

---

32. Gaadsan, another group of the Biyamaal clan grouping live in the Western Somaliland.
33. Hassan Osman Ahmed, "La Cittá di Marka, I Biimaal e il Dominio sulla Costa Somala, pp.80-1.

was reluctant to increase its involvement and responsibility over its colony.

Following this humiliation, it was no surprise when Filonardi announced his resignation on 3 December.[34] In spite of this, he continued to function for his government up to the expiration of the contract, by which time the Italian government had signed a new contract with Console Antonio Cecchi, who created the Societá Anonima Commerciale Italiana del Benadir, known as the Societá del Benadir, on 15 April 1896.[35]

As Marka had now become the rebel city, the Italian authorities avoided sending commissioners there. Giacomo Trevis, the Resident in Baraawa (Brava) at that time, was to oversee Marka.

In early November 1895, Marka was again subjected to repressive action, when the Somalis killed recruits to the Italian administration. In reaction, the Biyamaal besieged Marka and again cut its communications with the interior. The deepening conflict resulted in the killing of Trevis.[36] Italy's plan to create a territory of settlement for Italian emigration in southern Somaliland was failing to be viable.

Italy's Futile Attempts

The Biyamaal resistance and their sieges of Marka, and the Italian authority's retribution, continued unabated for many years. It was heightened when, in November 1896,

---

34. Ibid., p.83.
35. Ibid., p.85.
36. Ibid., p.93. Few months before his death Giacomo Trevis became Marka Resident.

while on a pleasure trip, Console Antonio Cecchi, the Societá del Benadir administrator and also the *de facto* governor of Southern Somaliland, and his lieutenants, were ambushed at Lafoole, a small village a few kilometres from Afgooye, south of Muqdisho, by Wa'daan and Biyamaal fighters, who killed 14 of them, including Cecchi. In reprisal the Italian authority burned all villages of the Wa'daan clans and arrested and deported Marka elders, including those of the Biyamaal clan. The Biyamaal and Wa'daan fighters again began their siege of Marka and this time tightened their grip over the port city. After futile attempts by the Italians to break the blockade, they finally bent to the demands of the fighters by releasing the Marka elders.

In spite of the fact that they thwarted the colonialists' attempts to take their land, the Biyamaal and Wa'daan resistance were not properly organised. Nevertheless, they confronted the sophisticated army of a colonial power with their indigenous defensive tools and will. In spite of the Somalis' high casualities and loss, they had prevented the intruders from reaching west of the river Shabeelle for all these years.

Reform of Biyamaal and Wa'daan Resistance

In the first decade Biyamaal and Wa'daan resistance was directed against colonial exploitation of their land. Then, between the end of 1906 and the early part of 1907 that of the Biyamaal assumed a form of organized resistance. Under the leadership of Ma'alim Mursal Abdi Yusuf[37] and Sheekh Abikar Gafle, the resistance was transformed from

---

37. Ma-alim literary means teacher of Islamic teachings.

just a clannic resistance to one based on Islamic principles. Sheikh Abikar and Ma'alim Mursal crusaded widely against the intruders. The aim was to widen the struggle against all the intruders and infidel.[38] The change reflected a clear influence of the nationalistic Daraawiish movement which was opposing British and Abyssinian intrusion in the Somali peninsula (see below). For the first time, their military tactics were changing as a result of modern weapons and perhaps of Daraawiish military advisers.

On 5 March 1905 Italy signed a peace agreement and protection treaty with the Daraawiish at Ilig, in the north-eastern part of Somaliland. The Ilig Treaty recognised Sayid Mahamed as the ruler of the Nugaal Valley (Appendix III). By assigning the Nugaal Valley to the Daraawiish state, Italy hoped to eliminate the threat of the Daraawiish moving into their dominion in Benaadir. Italy was concerned about its colony in Benaadir and believed that the object of the Daraawiish struggle to be southern Somaliland, where they could find abundance of water.

As Italy's attempt to contain the Daraawiish influence in the north was failing, the Biyamaal resistance, inspired by religious fervour, was receiving new momentum. To counter the new threat Italy decided to reinforce its troops and use all means to suppress the resistance.

In early February 1907 Lieutenant Pesenti, a young Italian officer new to the colony, and his troops ventured to interrupt a local meeting and arrest the local leaders in Moyaale, east of the river Shabeelle. In a counter-attack Biyamaal fighters

---

38. Hassan Osman Ahmed, "La Cittá di Marka, I Biimaal e il Dominio sulla Costa Somala, p.137.

destroyed Italian position at Dhanaane. In reaction, the Italian troops razed all villages in a nearly hundred-kilometre range, killed people and seized animals.[39]

The Dhanaane clash was a turning point in Italian involvement in the Benaadir area, as it accelerated the arrival of the new governor, Tommaso Carletti, who arrived in Muqdisho in May 1907.

On the one hand, Italy was now intent on reinforcing its forces in southern Somaliland and bulldozing the resistance, on the other, Governor Carletti was instructed to start 'pacifying' the people in order to enable him to penetrate the interior, an area which Italy had not hitherto entered.[40]

Despite fierce resistance, from July 1908 Italian colonial authority began to thrust its way to the west of the river Shabeelle. Under the command of Major Antonio Di Giorgio, Italian forces, reinforced with an Eritrean contingent, started to overwhelm the rebels with utmost savagery, burning any village suspected of nurturing opposition.

THE DARAAWIISH RESISTANCE

Somali resistance to foreign interference in their lives dated back to at least the years between 1528 and 1535 when, under the command of Imam Ahmed (Ahmed Ibn Ibrahim al-Ghazi), known as Ahmed 'Gurey' (the left-handed), the Somali devastated, and for a time successfully pushed back

---

39. Ibid., p.138.
40. Ibid., p.139.

the Abyssinian Empire. It was only with the help of the Portuguese[41] that the Abyssinians defeated the Somali forces.

The resistance to colonial interference which Sayid Mahamed Abdulle Hassan inspired and led at the close of the nineteenth century and for the succeeding two decades was nationalistic in essence, and in a tradition not seen in the Somali peninsula since Ahmed Gurey's war against Abyssinia in the sixteenth century.

At the end of the nineteenth century, Islam was reawakening in Eastern Africa, as a result of a revival of Islam in the Muslim world.[42] This tendency might have been triggered by the Euro-Christian colonisation of Muslim lands in Africa and Asia, creating a widespread reaction culminating in a resurgence of a revivalist movement against the Euro-Christian hegemony. The Mahdist revolt in the Sudan in 1880s and that of the Darwiish (Dervish) movement led by Sayid Mahamed in Somalia during the same period, are examples of this revivalist movement.[43]

The resistance led by Sayid Mahamed Abdulle was motivated by religious and cultural principles. His objective was to establish his suzerainty 'over the whole of the Somali territory'.[44]

Islam served as the ideology of the Darwiish movement. A Darwiish is a Muslim believer who takes vows of poverty

---

41. Isabel Burton, ed., *First Footsteps in East Africa by Captain Sir Richard F. Burton, op. cit.*, p.10.
42. Abdi Sheikh-Abdi, *Divine Madness*, 1992, pp.36-7.
43. Ibid., pp.36-40
44. Jardine, D., *The Mad Mullah of Somaliland*, 1923, p.159.

to lead a life of austerity in the service of Allah and of his community.

A Brief Background to Sayid Mahamed's Life

Sayid Mahamed was born in the Sa'madeeqa valley, a small watering place between Wud-Wud and Buuhodle in 1856,[45] during a spring season known as Gobaysane.[46] Two influences left an impression on the life of the Sayid. The first influence was Islamic study, the other the might of pastoralism.

At the age of seven he attended Qoranic school and at eleven he learned the 114 *suras* of the Qoran by heart. Afterwards he became a teacher. After two years of teaching the Qoran, he began to question his faith, a crisis that took him in search of more rigorous religious learning for ten years. He travelled to many Islamic seats of learning, including Muqdisho (Mugadisho), Nairobi, Harar and Khartoum (Sudan), where he sought out the most learned *sheikhs* in each place.

In his thirties he set off for Mecca to discharge his *haj* obligations.[47] While in Mecca, he met Sheikh Mohammed Salah (1853-1917), who changed the young Mahamed Abdulle Hassan completely. The mystic Sheikh Mohammed Salah of Sudan was the founder of the Salahiya order[48] which was

---

45. Aw-Jaamac Cumar Ciise, *Taariikhdii Daraawiishta iyo Sayid Maxamed Cabdulle Xasan, (1895-1921),* 1976, p.4. Others believe that he was born in 1864.
46. Traditionally, Somalis name seasons for events or their effect. Gobaysane was famous for its abundance.
47. *Haj* is one of the five pillars of Islam. Every Muslim is required to do *haj*, in Mecca, at least once in his lifetime.
48. Salihiya is an offshoot of Ahmadiya order.

spreading in the Arabian peninsula and across the Red Sea into East Africa.

Islam has always had an association with brotherhoods (*dariqa*, literally meaning 'the way'), which express a mystical view of the Muslim faith. In the nineteenth century various religious organisations developed in Somalia to the extent that 'Somali profession of the Islamic faith was synonymous with membership of a sufi brotherhood'.[49]

The Sufi order grew out of the main Qadiriya order, founded by Sheikh Abdul-Qadir Jilani in the twelfth century. However, in later centuries sufist sectarianism evolved which could be categorised in three groups of Muslim fellowship: (i) the resisters who believed in struggle, (ii) the moderates who usually went about their pedagogical teaching but occasionally created rebellion, and (iii) the conservatives who practised their mystic meditation without concern for their social environment, sometimes collaborating with the rulers of the country.[50]

In 1895, following his sojourn in Arabia, Sayid Mahamed Abdulle Hassan returned to Somaliland with a mandate to be the Salahiya representative.[51] On his arrival in Berbera port, Sayid Mahamed refused to pay a tax to the customs. His arrival home coincided with the introduction of a new

---

49. I M Lewis, *A Modern History of Somalia*, 1980, p.63.
50. Bradford G. Martin, "Muslim Politics and Resistance to Colonial Rule", in *Journal of African History*, 10,3 (1969), pp.471-86.
51. Aw-Jaamac Cumar Ciise, *Taariikhdii Daraawiishta iyo Sayid Maxamed Cabdulle Xasan, (1895-1921), op. cit.*, p. 8. About the mandate is in dispute. Others believe that the other *hajis* who accompanied him in the *haj* recommended him to represent Salihiya in Somalia.

tax system by the British Consul General, Colonel James Haya Sadler.[52] The Sayid objected to paying customs duties to a foreign power since he was entering his own land. The story goes that, when the customs officer decided to arrest him, a well-intended interpreter explained away the sheikh's refusal to pay as insanity: "Sir, he mad mullah,"[53] and thereby originated the label of Mad Mullah which colonial literature later assigned to the Sayid.

Before the return of Sayid Mahamed in British Somaliland the influence of Andarawiya, which like the Salihiya is an offshoot of Ahmadiya,[54] was limited. The Qadiriya settlements were well established both here and on the Benaadir coast in the south. In Berbera Sayid Mahamed established a base from which he campaigned and spread the Salahiya order while at the same time condemning the Qadiriya's moral laxity[55] in accommodating colonialism.

---

52. Said S. Samatar, *Oral Poetry and Somali Nationalism, op. cit.*, p.106.
53. Aw-Jaamac Cumar Ciise, *Taariikhdii Daraawiishta iyo Sayid Maxamed Cabdulle Xasan, (1895-1921), op.cit.*, p.9. There is another version of how the Sayid acquired this epithet. It says when he left Mecca, he passed the port of Aden. The Sheikh had a skirmish with an English officer. An interpreter named Ali Qaje explained to the officer by saying, "Sir, pardon, he Mad Mullah".
54. Ahmadiya was founded by Ahmad bin Idris Al-Faasi (1760-1837) in Mecca, Saudi Arabia.
55. Said S. Samatar, *Oral Poetry and Somali Nationalism, op. cit.*, p.106. The Qadiriya *dariiqa* was founded by Sheikh 'Abdul-Qadir Jilani (d. AD 1166) and buried in Baghdad. It was divided into two groups: Zayla'iya, named after its founder Sheikh Cabdiraxmaan Zaylici (Sheikh Abdul-Rahman Az-Zayli'i, d. 1883), in the north. Uwaysiya named after its founder Sheikh Uways Mahamed (Sheikh

Sayid Mahamed's attempt to proselytise and convert urban Somalis to the Salahiya order, however, met with stiff resistance from the Berbera community. There was firm opposition from the Qadiriya order which had established roots in the area. His conflict with the town's religious men caused him to lose the sympathy of Berbera people.[56] In turn, Berbera *culama* (theologians) fought back to discredit him and his new order. To further undermine him, they informed the administration of his intentions.[57]

The rift between the two *dariiqas* intensified when the British administration sided with Qadiriya and closed down the Salahiya religious centre at the end of 1897. This infuriated Sayid Mahamed, who later moved with his small group of followers to his maternal home, among the Dhulbahante, in the south of British Somaliland.

The Beginning of the Daraawiish Struggle

After being forced to leave Berbera, Sayid Mahamed moved to Qorya-weyn in the south of British Somaliland, where he began preaching Islam under the Salahiya banner. In spite of failing to convince the urbanised Berbera residents, he

---

Uways Bin Mahammad al-Baraawa) killed in 1909 by the Daraawiish forces in Biyooley in the south Somaliland.

56. Ibid, p.107.

57. Aw-Jaamac Cumar Ciise, *Taariikhdii Daraawiishta iyo Sayid Maxamed Cabdulle Xasan, (1895-1921), op. cit.*, p.12. Aw-Gaas Ahmed was the one who brought Sayid Mahamed to the attention of the administration about Sayid Mahamed's by saying "This sheikh is planning something. If you do not arrest him now, you will look for him very far." (Wadaadkaas waxbuu soo wadaa. Haddaan haatan la qabanna meel fog baa laga dooni doonaa).

found willing listeners in the pastoral society uninfluenced by an urban lifestyle.

The Sayid started to settle clan disputes thus acquiring the reputation of peacemaker, and began to be seen by the pastoralists as an *awliyo* (saint) who had been sent among them.[58] In the first period, the British administration welcomed his exercise of authority and saw him as an ally.[59] But his aims to mediate and unify clans were in order to gain their support in the fight against the intruders, and it soon became evident that his aspirations were to oppose colonial interests. An incident that happened around this time, in 1899, proved a turning point in the relations between the Sayid and the British authority. A British administration constable, an *ilaalo*, went to the Daraawiish settlement and sold his gun to the Sayid.[60] On his return to Berbera the constable reported that his gun had been stolen by the Sayid. The case prompted the British administration to send a letter to Sayid Mahamed ordering him to surrender the stolen gun immediately, but instead, on 1 September 1899, Sayid Mahamed replied in a letter challenging British rule in the country. This defiance brought the Sheikh to the attention of Britain itself, and the episode soured British attitudes towards the Sayid and his movement. The conflict between the Daraawiish movement and the colonial powers which was to last for two decades had begun.

In August 1898, the Daraawiish occupied Burao', the centre of British Somaliland, and by doing this, Sayid Mahamed

---

58. Ibid, p.14.
59. Douglas Jardine, *The Mad Mullah of Somaliland*, 1932, p.86.
60. I M Lewis, *A Modern History of Somalia, op. cit.*, p. 68.

established control over the watering places of the local clans, namely the Habar Yonis and the Habar Tol je'le clans.[61] He engaged in some peace-making between Habar Yonis and Habar Tol je'le clans, and between the Dhulbahante and Habar Tol je'le.[62] A huge assembly was held in Burao' at which Sayid Mahamed urged the congregation to initiate a *jihad* (holy war) against the Ethiopians, British and Italians who had come to colonise the Somali territory.

Further differences began appearing during this period. Sultan Nuur Ahmed Ammaan, sultan of the Habar Yonis clan, felt uneasy about the leadership of Sayid Mahamed. Sultan Nuur could do little to end it alone, therefore, he sought British help. With this knowledge the Sayid was able to undermine the sultan's leadership, and persuaded the Habar Yonis clan to depose their leader[63] and replace him with one who was favourable to the Daraawiish cause. Sultan Nuur was deposed and replaced by Sultan Madar who, however, was soon opposing Sayid Mahamed.[64] Obtaining leadership sympathetic to the Daraawiish cause within the Somali clans became one of the principal policies of the Sayid.

Shortly afterwards, the Daraawiish raided a Qadiriya settlement at Sheikh, a small town between Berbera and Burao', and massacred its inhabitants. Panic spread in Berbera where an imminent Daraawiish attack was feared. Surprised by the new development, the British authority started to take

---

61. Saadia Touval, *Somali Nationalism. op. cit.* ,p.52.
62. I M Lewis, *A Modern History of Somalia*, op. cit., p. 69.
63. Ibid., p.69.
64. Sadia Muuse Ahmed, field note, interviewed on 25th August 1993, London, England.

the Daraawiish activities seriously. However, by the end of 1899, the British were occupied by the Boer War and could do little to contain the spread of the Daraawiish movement, which was badly hindering their trade with the interior of the territory under their administration.

The British administration in Berbera urged their government to take action. It did not take long for London to consent to raise a local levy of troops who would attempt to suppress the spread of the Daraawiish movement.

During the same period, Sayid Mahamed preached the Salahiya philosophy and the practice of *tawassul* — the veneration of saints. He taught chanting and the praise of Sheikh Mohammed Salah by singing "Shay Lillah Sheikh Mahamed Salah." He gave the name Daraawiish to the adherents of his Salahiya *dariqa* (order) and introduced the wearing of a white turban (*duub cad*) which was also customary sufi costume. Within a short time many pastoral communities followed the Daraawiish. In 1898 the Daraawiish followers numbered more than 5000 men and women with 200 rifles. In the middle of April 1898, the Daraawiish moved their base to Dareema-addo, a watering place north-west of Buuhodle.

From Movement to State

Within a short time the Daraawiish grew in men, power and wealth. Because of this growth, it became necessary for Sayid Mahamed to institutionalise the movement by creating four main governmental apparatuses.[65] At the top

---

65. Aw-Jaamac Cumar Ciise, *Taariikhdii Daraawiishta iyo Sayid Maxamed Cabdulle Xasan*, (1895-1921), op.cit., p.126.

there was the ministerial Council (*qusuusi*) which presided over affairs of state; next came bodyguards (*gaar-haye*) who were responsible for the security of senior members; third was the regular army (*Maara-weyn*) which was organised into seven regiments: Sheekhyaale, Gola-weyne, Taar-gooye, Indha-badan, Miinanle, Dharbash and Rag-xun, each with its commandant (*muqaddim*), and varying between 1000 to 4000 men; and fourth and finally was the civilian population (*Reer-beede*) consisting mainly of people from clans who followed the Daraawiish movement.

By forming a standing army, the movement had to face pressing needs such as food and other logistical requirements of the troops. In the first period they were supported by voluntary charity (*siyaaro*) which Muslims are required to give to religious men. However, as the needs of the army increased, the Daraawiish began to lobby for more help for 'the state'. On the other hand, they spread rumours that anybody who did not help the Daraawiish in the *jihad* struggle was not Muslim and must be killed and his property confiscated.[66]

The Daraawiish structure could be considered to constitute a state, since the three salient features of state are defined as territory, population living in that defined territory, and a government which is sovereign to rule the country and the people. Though fluid, all these characteristics can be identified in the Daraawiish.

Such a state was fashioned on the model of the Salahiya brotherhood, with strict hierarchy and rigid centralisation by a religious order. The cohesive force of the Daraawiish

---

66. Ibid., p.23.

state polity was based on religious ideology, and was a radical departure from the politics of clan alliance.

Some followed it with enthusiasm, some with caution, but soon many conflicts began to develop. Garaad Ali Garaad Mahamud, Sultan of Bah-Ararsame Dhulbahante clan, whose people lived in Nugaal, felt uneasy at the expanding power of the Sayid among his matrilineal relatives of the Dhulbahante. Towards the end of 1899, Sayid Mahamed sent a delegation to the Garaad to try and persuade him and his people to join the Daraawiish state. He sent a further delegation to the Garaad inviting him to the *xarun* (headquarters). With reluctance Garaad Ali accepted, and in the heated debate which followed Garaad Ali emphasised his position in the following way,

I am the ruler of Nugaal and its people. Their management is mine and I expect everybody to respect it.[67]

This inevitably led to a confrontation between two systems: the traditionalist against the new. The Daraawiish practice was alien to pastoral society. Traditionally the clan is the most important political unit of the Somalis and this clashed with the new system introduced by the Sayid.

The resulting hostility prompted Sayid Mahamed to dispatch a group of Daraawiish to assassinate the Garaad.

The killing of Garaad Ali stunned the Somali clans and destabilised the Daraawiish.[68] This incident proved to be one of the most catastrophic miscalculations made by Sayid

---

67. Ibid., p.25. This is what he said in Somali, "Nugaal iyo dadka deggan anaa Boqor u ah. Taladooda nin iiga dambeeya maahee ninna uga dambayn maayo!".
68. Ibid., p.26.

Mahamed. Many of his followers left him. Only his maternal kin, Ali Geri, stood by him. Having lost the support of the Nugaal people, Sayid Mahamed and his followers were forced to flee to Western Somaliland, to his paternal kin.

The Battles Between The Daraawiish and The Colonialists

The Daraawiish had a military organisation that was expert in guerrilla warfare. By drawing their enemies to ideal terrain, they used to strike at will. The British, sometimes with their allies, sent one expedition after another. The first expedition left Burao' on 22 May 1901, and consisted of 21 officers of the British and Indian armies and a levy of 1500 Somalis. Between 1900 and 1904, four British expeditions were sent against the Daraawiish. Well-known battles were Afbakayle, which took place on 3 June 1901, Fardhidin on 16 July 1901, Beerdhiga (Eeragoo) on 4 April 1901, Agaarweyne (Gumburo) on April 1903, Daratoole on 22 April 1903, Jidbaale on 10 January 1904 and Ruugga (Dulmadoobe) on 9 August 1913.[69]

During the first period, the Daraawiish won many battles because of their experience of guerrilla warfare, their knowledge of the territory and adaptability to the environment, their belief that they were fighting a *jihad* (holy war) and therefore a just war, and their military organisation. However, after many successes over the intruders, they changed their tactics of guerrilla warfare to conventional tactics. This change of strategy proved fatal for them.

---

69. See Aw-Jaamac Cumar Ciise, *Taariikhdii Daraawiishta iyo Sayid Maxamed Cabdulle Xasan*, (1895-1921), *op. cit.*, pp.41-102.

On 9 January 1904 on the plains of Jidbaale, a watering place north of Las Anod in the east of British Somaliland, they sought head on confrontation with the British. In the following battle, the Daraawiish lost between 7000 and 8000, dead or injured.[70] The defeat demoralised and disorganised the Daraawiish. With the British forces on their heels, the fleeing Daraawiish headed to the Majeerteen Sultanate in the north-east. On their way they sent a message to Boqor Osman, whose relationship with the Sayid was marred by a failed political marriage when the latter had asked to marry a daughter of Boqor Osman, Qaali.[71]

Meanwhile, the British asked the Italian Consulate in Aden to press Boqor Osman not to give the Sayid sanctuary. Boqor Osman gave way to Italian and British pressure, and declined to give refuge to the frustrated Daraawiish. This angered Sayid Mahamed at a time when many of his followers were deserting. Consequently, fighting erupted between the Daraawiish and the forces of Boqor Osman. The Daraawiish forces were obliged to head for Ilig, a strategic place on the Indian Ocean, in the northeast of Somaliland.

The Ilig Treaty

After four years of fighting, the British found that they could not annihilate the Daraawiish as they had believed. Because of financial troubles and opposition at home, in 1904 they had been compelled to change tactics and make

---

70. Said S. Samatar, *Oral Poetry and Somali Nationalism, op. cit.*, p.155.
71. Aw-Jaamac Cumar Ciise, *Taariikhdii Daraawiishta iyo Sayid Maxamed Cabdulle Xasan*, (1895-1921), *op. cit.*, p.63.

peace with the Daraawiish through the Italians - who had not been in military conflict with the Daraawiish. Haji Abdille Shihiri, who was a Daraawiish confidant, became the mediator between the Italians and the Daraawiish. Haji Abdille Shihiri met with Cavalier Giulio Pestalozza, the Diplomatic Representative of the Italian Government at Aden, where he took a letter for the Sayid.

Craving respite, the Sayid accepted negotiation with the Italians who proposed that he rule the territory from Ayl and Garaad on the Indian Ocean to Nugaal in the interior. The agreement included a condition to release Sultan Yusuf Ali Kenadid, Sultan of Hobyo (Obbia), who had been deposed and imprisoned by the Italians after he refused to let British forces disembark at Hobyo with the intention of attacking the Daraawiish from the east while other British forces engaged with the Daraawiish at Cagaar-weyne (Gumburo) on 17 April 1903. As a result of his refusal, Sultan Yusuf Ali was deported to Assab in Eritrea in 1903.[72]

After heated negotiations an agreement was reached on 5 March 1905. Giulio Pestalozza signed for Italy. At Berbera on the 24th March 1905, a provisional Agreement was signed by the British and by representatives of the Daraawiish, declaring amongst other things, that the Agreement between Italy and the Daraawiish was in accord with the views of the British government.[73]

---

72. Ibid., pp.117-18. On this occasion the Sayid said, "Talyan Koofiyad weynow, dabadeed aad kalaantoo. Kidibkii aad shubtee, Keenadiid ma waddaa?" Translated in English, "O Italian with big hat, talk later. Did you bring with you Keenadiid?"
73. Somali Republic, *The Somali Peninsula: A New Light on Imperial Motives*, 1962, pp.120-121.

The Ilig Treaty recognised Sayid Mahamed as leader of a mini state in the Nugaal Valley, under the protection of Italy (Appendix III). It also accorded him religious liberty and freedom of trade, except in arms and slaves.[74]

By assigning the Nugaal Valley as a Daraawiish state, Italy hoped to eliminate the threat of the Daraawiish to influence and support revolt in their own domain of Benaadir.[75] However, on receiving the news of the Daraawiish' status, the Biyamaal and Wa'daan clans rebelled against Italian rule. Only after Italy bombarded Marka did the Italians subdue the Biyamaal uprising.[76]

Master of Eloquence

Knowing that the colonialists could not be defeated by force alone, Sayid Mahamed began to change strategy by beginning to use words as arms. Just as words, spoken or written, have been the most powerful means of communication of mankind,[77] he consummately and skilfully used the medium of Somali verse. He repeatedly sought to gain in verse what he could not succeeded in acquiring with arms. When he lost a battle, he "dipped into his reservoir of rhymes to encourage his shattered army."[78] He designed his verse to enhance his

---

74. For more detail of the agreement see Aw-Jaamac Cumar Ciise, *Taariikhdii Daraawiishta iyo Sayid Maxamed Cabdulle Xasan*, (1895-1921), *op. cit.*, p.134.
75. Robert L Hess, *Italian Colonialism in Somalia*, 1966, p.134.
76. Ibid., pp.45-46.
77. Mahamed D. Afrax, "The Mirror of Culture," in *The Somali Challenge*, ed. Ahmed I. Samatar, 1994, pp.233-249.
78. Quoted in Said S. Samatar, *Oral Poetry and Somali Nationalism*, *op. cit.*, p.181.

cause, to encourage his followers or scorn and discredit his enemies. However, by scorning his enemies, he sometimes preached the pastoral ethos excessively like an "epigram that borders on the obscene."[79]

The period in Ilig was, by concensus, the period during which he composed his best poems: dextrously using the Somali language which is well noted for its richness of vocabulary;[80] using the medium of poetry as high powered propaganda warfare, Sayid Mahamed became a "literary master".[81] As poetry is the principle medium of mass communication, his mastery of the art won him the reputation of being the greatest Somali poet, and earned him the description "master of eloquence"[82] from one modern-day admirer.

> The Sayid appealed to a traditional code of ethics that he knew would strike a responsive chord in the [hearts of those who heard them]. The notion of unbending defiance in the face of calamitous circumstances was a theme he often stressed in his poems... Yet these tactics, designed to hold the ranks of the faithful together, concealed the real shift in strategy that the Sayid was initiating in the light of grim realities.[83]

---

79. Ibid., p.153.
80. Cali Xirsi Cartan, note field, interviewed on 22 August 1993, London, England.
81. B. W. Andrezejewski and I. M. Lewis, *Somali Poetry*, 1964, p.74.
82. Spencer J. Trimingham, *Islam in Ethiopia, 1952*, p.34.
83. Said S. Samatar, *Oral Poetry and Somali Nationalism, op. cit.*, p.143.

Long years of adversity gave vitality to Sayid Mahamed's personality. He was persisting in the face of overwhelming odds. In spite of his totalitarianism and storming character, his tyranny was directed towards a noble end[84] as his objective was to get rid of colonial power.

The Reconstruction of the Daraawiish State

The peace agreement gave the Sayid a period of respite to recover his strength and influence. He built up his forces and, in breach of the treaty, imported arms on an unprecedented scale.

He set up a well-coordinated strategy to sabotage the colonial administration and to terrorise and destabilise clans that he saw as loyal to British and Italian rule, those under the Majeerteen and the Hobyo Sultanates, and Ogaadeen clans, by sending out roving bands of raiders (*burcad*)[85]. He invaded Mudug to establish contact with Bah-Geri on the upper Shabeelle and extended his attacks on the Hobyo Sultanate.

Indiscriminate raiding, seizing and plundering of the property of fellow Muslims, and breaking a solemn treaty - even though with infidels - were seen as dishonourable, and alienated Sayid Mahamed from many from among his followers.

---

84. I M Lewis, *A Modern History of Somalia, op. cit.*, p.82. See Drake-Brockman and Ralph E., *British Somaliland*, p.5-20. See D. Jardine, *The Mad Mullah*, 1923, pp.314-316.
85. Aw-Jaamac Cumar Ciise, *Taariikhdii Daraawiishta iyo Sayid Mahamed Cabdulle Xasan*, (1895-1921), *op. cit.*, p.20.

At the end of 1909 the Daraawiish moved first to Adaydheero then two years later to Dameero and later still to Taleh. At Taleh, the heart of the Nugaal valley, the Daraawiish reunited and started to build impressive and strategic garrisons. Taleh was ideally placed as it was at the centre between the western Hawd (Haud), the Red Sea in the east, the Indian Ocean, the Majeerteen and Hobyo Sultanates to the south, and British Somaliland to the north. It was abundant with water and pasture. There the Daraawiish built four garrisons: Silsilad could take two thousand fighters and five thousand animals; Falaad, was the headquarters for the Sayid and his advisers; Daawad was for guests; and Eegi or Daar-Ilaalo was an outpost for the headquarters.[86]

Although the building of the fortress gave the Daraawiish the appearance of supremacy in the area, it was also a complete contradiction of the guerrilla warfare tactics that the Daraawiish had adopted in previous years, and would give the enemy a fixed target to attack and a defined territory for battle.

However, after the failure of another peace attempt by the British with the Daraawiish in November 1909, London ordered its colonial administration in the British Somaliland to confine themselves to three coastal towns on the Red Sea: Berbera, Zeyla' and Bullahar.[87] This decision resulted in declining British prestige in the country.

---

86. Ibid., p.204.
87. The order might have been from W. Churchill, the then Under-Secretary of State for Colonies who came to visit Berbera. See Aw-Jaamac Cumar Ciise, *Taariikhdii Daraawiishta iyo Sayid Maxamed Cabdulle Xasan, (1895-1921), op. cit.,* p.166.

By 1913 the Daraawiish dominated the entire hinterland of the Somali peninsula. In the new status quo, the Daraawiish became the only organised institution in the area,[88] and as a result, the booming trade of the British-controlled coastal area with the hinterland became completely at the mercy of the Daraawiish. This prompted the British to revise their policy, and they formed a mobile force, the Camel Corps, to police the immediate hinterlands. Under the command of the arrogant and tough Colonel Richard Corfield, the Camel Corps soon began to patrol in the immediate hinterland.

The Daraawiish's Diplomatic Victories

On the diplomatic front, Sayid Mahamed made an alliance with the new Ethiopian Emperor, Lij Iyasu, who acceded to the throne in December 1913. Emperor Iyasu was sympathetic to Islam and moved his court to Dire Dawa among his Muslim subjects.[89] He aspired to create a Muslim empire in East Africa. To fulfil his dream, he proposed to make an alliance with Sayid Mahamed. It is probable that he supplied financial aid and arms to the Daraawiish, and sent a German arms technician, called Emil Kirsch, to Taleh to help the Daraawiish state.

The fear of an alliance of Ethiopian Muslims and the Daraawiish alarmed the European capitals as well as the Ethiopian orthodox church. Their concern was justified as the announcement of Emperor Iyasu's conversion to

---

88. Siciid Mahamed Guure, field note, interviewed in March 1977, Iskushuban (Bari Region), Somalia.
89. Aw-Jaamac Cumar Ciise, *Taariikhdii Daraawiishta iyo Sayid Mahamed Cabdulle Xasan, (1895-1921), op. cit.*, p.78.

Islam was made in April 1916.[90] However, before he could consolidate his power, Emperor Iyasu was deposed on 27 September 1916.

On another diplomatic front, Sayid Mahamed made an alliance with the Ottoman Empire.[91] However, in 1917, the Italians apprehended Sheikh Ahmed Shirwa Mahamed and found in his possession a document from the Turkish government giving assurance of their support and recognising Sayid Mahamed as the Amir of Somaliland.[92]

The diplomatic achievements, the Ilig Treaty, the British withdrawal to the coast, and the reconstruction of the Daraawiish state in the heart of the country helped to enhance the prestige of Sayid Mahamed throughout Somaliland. But his success had disadvantages as it made the Sayid over-confident which in turn caused him to evaluate falsely the strategy of his enemies. He over estimated the help he could receive from Emperor Iyasu, who had only a short time left in power, and from the Ottoman Empire which was in decline.

The Annihilation of the Daraawiish State

During the great days of the Daraawiish state in the Nugaal Valley, *qusuusi* (advisers) of the state recommended that farming should stop, and trading with the coast should be halted to avert enemy spies from reporting about the

---

90. Robert L Hess, *Italian Colonialism in Somalia*, op. cit., p.146.
91. For the agreement see Francesco Caroselli, *Ferro e Fuoco in Somalia*, 1931, p.224. For more detail see also Aw-Jaamac Cumar Ciise, *Taariikhdii Daraawiishta iyo Sayid Maxamed Cabdulle Xasan*, (1895-1921), *op. cit.*, pp.242-246.
92. I M Lewis, *A Modern History of Somalia*, op. cit., p.78.

Daraawiish.[93] They suggested moving the headquarters to a location where rival informants could not spy on them. Sayid Mahamed accepted the advice without examining the possible consequences. In mid-1918 the headquarters were transferred to Mirashi[94], a mountainous place with difficult access for their enemies.[95] However, that decision proved detrimental to the Daraawiish tactics as it interrupted communication with their other settlements. During this period the Daraawiish knew little about their enemies' preparations.[96]

While the Daraawiish were in this isolated situation, the British built up their fire power which they reinforced with the aeroplane, a newly invented lethal weapon, with which they started to attack all Daraawiish bases in Taleh and Mirashi simultaneously on the 21 January 1920. This took the Daraawiish military leaders by surprise. Their plans never included a strategy to protect their bases against such fantastic weapons. On 3 February 1920 the British captured Taleh, and the Daraawiish troops abandoned their forts in the Nugaal Valley and other areas before fleeing to Western Somaliland. There they regrouped when a natural disaster occurred. Smallpox broke out in the region and decimated the men and livestock.

Meanwhile, the British Governor despatched a peace delegation to Sayid Mahamed pressing him to surrender. In exchange he was to be allowed to establish his own religious

---

93. Aw-Jaamac Cumar Ciise, *Taariikhdii Daraawiishta iyo Sayid Maxamed Cabdulle Xasan*, (1895-1921), *op. cit.*, p.260.
94. Ibid., p.261-262.
95. Ibid., p.262.
96. Ibid., p.206.

settlement in the west of British Somaliland. Nonetheless, Sayid Mahamed categorically refused to surrender, and to prove to the British authority that the Daraawiish was still capable of intimidating its subjects, raided Isaaq clansmen grazing their livestock near the Ethiopian border. The attack outraged the Isaaq clans, and with the help of the administration, a force of Isaaq men led by Haji Warsame Bullale, known as Haji Warabe, staged a massive onslaught on the already feeble Daraawiish.

After this fatal blow Sayid Mahamed and some of his *qusuusi* members fled to Imay, in the Arusi country in Ethiopia. After arriving in Imay, the Sayid and his remaining companions started to build thirteen new garrisons but Sayid Mahamed did not live long enough to realise the reconstruction of the Daraawiish state. He succumbed to an attack of influenza on 21 December 1920 at the age of fifty-six.

With the fear of the Daraawiish eliminated, the Italian colonial power was set to establish its rule over the rest of what would became the Italian Somaliland. Currently controlling only Benaadir, Italy now set as its top priority the elimination of the north-eastern sultanates.

THE NORTH-EASTERN SOMALILAND SULTANATES

The north-eastern sultanates of Majeerteen and Hobyo developed a very effective political organization with diversified measures of centralized authority over relatively large territories. Italy, Britain, Germany and France had been trying to solicit them into their sphere of influence since the early days of their competion for the Somali peninsula.

In the closing decades of the 1880s Germany was the first colonial power to have built a special relationship with the Majeerteen.

To the other colonial powers' surprise however, on 7 April 1889, it was Italy who concluded a treaty of protection with the Majeerteen sultanate, having only a few months before, in December 1888, signed a similar treaty with the Hobyo sultanate.[97] The protectorate agreements were renewed by the Majeerteen on 7 April 1895 and on 11 April 1895 by the Hobyo.

The treaty terms clearly stipulated that Italy was not to interfere in the internal affairs of the sultanates,[98] and in order to promote the Italian Government and the sultanates' interests, Italy agreed to send commissioners to both sultanates.

By accepting Italy's protection in December 1888, Sultan Yusuf Ali of Hobyo was planning to use Italy's support in his dispute with the Sultan of Zanzibar over the border region north of Warsheekh. He was also interested in using this support against Boqor Osman of the Majeerteen Sultanate with whom he contested control over the Nugaal Valley. As a countermove against Sultan Yusuf Ali, Boqor Osman Mahamud also accepted Italy's protection. They had both signed the protectorate agreements for their own expansionist objectives, and, by exploiting the conflicting interests among competing powers, to avoid direct occupation of their territories by force.

However, the relationship between Hobyo and Italy was complicated when Sultan Yusuf Ali refused the Italian proposal

---

97. Robert L Hess, *Italian Colonialism in Somalia*, 1966, pp.24-28.
98. Cesare Maria De Vecchi, *Orizzonti d'Impero*, pp.56-7.

to sanction a British contingent of troops to disembark at Hobyo to pursue their battle with the Daraawiish (see above) in April 1903. Because of this controversy, Sultan Yusuf Ali and his son Yusuf Ali were eventually deposed by the Italians and deported to Assab in Eritrea[1]

Conflict of Interest

The sultanate of Majeerteen lay on the utmost tip of the Horn. To the north was the Red Sea, in the east there was the Indian Ocean. To the south of Majeerteenia stretched the Nugaal Valley. To the west British Somaliland.

To define their zone of influence, the Italian and British administrations signed the Anglo-Italian Treaty of 5 May 1894 which defined the Majeerteen Sultanate as being east of the 49° Meridian. The line fell to the east of Taleh and Baran. In 1906 Cavalier Pestalozza and General Swaine signed an agreement recognising Baran as under the Majeerteen sultanate.[2] Among other things, the Anglo-Italian treaty stipulated that the Italian government be responsible for any act committed by the Majeerteen against the people under British protection.[3] All these dealings were taking place behind the backs of the peoples concerned.

In March 1901, Boqor Osman extended his border by capturing two small towns in the Mudug region. The Mudug was an area regarded as Sultan Yusuf Ali's realm. As both sultans were under Italian protection, the contention prompted Giulio Pestalozza, the Italian Consul at Aden, to

---

1. Robert L Hess, *Italian Colonialism in Somalia*, pp.117-18.
2. Ibid., pp.76-80.
3. Ibid., p.91.

sail to Baargaal, the seat of the Majeerteen court, to press Boqor Osman to retreat and respect the treaties. Boqor Osman refused to give in.[4]

The matter worried Italy and it reasoned that unless Boqor Osman was brought under their directive they feared they could not control the sultanate. Misunderstanding and distrust was in the making. The conflict of interest was leading to confrontation as each side began accusing the other.

Whilst the situation was still in confusion, the Italian Minister in Cairo intercepted a letter from Boqor Osman seeking Ottoman protection over what the latter termed the "Independent Majeerteen Somali."[5] Furthermore, Italy learned about the sultanate's arms build-up. Before it was too late, Italy decided to breach the treaty and to bring Boqor Osman to his knees. The Volta ship bombarded the coastal villages of Bareeda and Bender Khassim (Boosaaso), crippling the sultanate's modest arms and ammunition warehouses. Boqor Osman fled to the interior, while Italian troops captured the sea towns of Alula, Bender Khassim, Bareeda and Muranyo. Boqor Osman had been taken by surprise, and had attempted unsuccessfully to counter the Italians in too many battlefields.

Things were further complicated by other developments in the region: the Italo-British arrangements for confining the Daraawiish to the Nugaal area was growing untenable. The British had failed to secure peace with the Daraawiish and were

---

4. Ibid. p.128.
5. Ibid., p.129.

in retreat.⁶ The good relationships which in the past Boqor Osman had had with Sayid Mahamed ended after persistent Daraawiish scorched earth raids on Majeerteen settlements. Initially Boqor Osman had repulsed invasions of his Sultanate by the Daraawiish. But armed confrontation with the Italians had made him vulnerable to the Daraawiish attacks. He turned to the Italians for an "honourable settlement".

Because of the Daraawiish threat to their Benaadir colony and the weakness of control afforded by the existing treaty with the Majeerteen, the Italians opted to open a dialogue with Boqor Osman. After long negotiations, in March 1910, they signed a renewal of the treaty but with a more rigid and effective protectorate powers and in their own interpretation.⁷

From Sovereign to Subject:
The Elimination of the North-Eastern Sultanates

The dawn of fascism in the early 1920s heralded a change of strategy for Italy as the north-eastern sultanates were soon to be forced within the boundaries of La Grande Somalia according to the plan of fascist Italy. With the arrival of Governor Cesare Maria De Vecchi on 15 December 1923 things began to change for that part of Somaliland. Italy had access to these parts under the successive protection treaties, but not direct rule. The fascist government had direct rule only over the Benaadir territory.

Given the defeat of the Daraawiish movement in the early 1920s and the rise of fascism in Europe, on 10 July 1925

---

6. Aw-Jaamac Cumar Ciise, *Taariikhdii Daraawiishta iyo Sayid Maxamed Cabdulle Xasan*, (1895-1921), p.166.
7. Robert L Hess, *Italian Colonialism in Somalia*, pp.141-2.

Benito Mussolini gave the green light to De Vecchi to start the takeover of the north-eastern sultanates.[8] Everything was to be changed and the treaties abrogated.

The real principles of colonialism meant possession and domination of the people, and the protection of the country from other greedy powers. Italy's interpretation of the treaties of protection with the north-eastern sultanates was comparable to her view of the Treaty of Uccialli with Abyssinia, and meant absolute control of the whole territory. Never mind that the subsequent tension between Abyssinia and Italy had culminated in 1896 in the battle of Adowa in which the Italians were overwhelmed and outmanoeuvred. The Italians had not learned their lesson, they were committing the same historical mistake.

Governor De Vecchi's first plan was to disarm the sultanates. But before the plan could be carried out there should be sufficient Italian troops in both sultanates. To make the enforcement of his plan more viable, he began to reconstitute the old Somali police corps, the Corpo Zaptié, as a colonial force.

Preparations for the Invasion

In preparation for the plan of invasion of the sultanates, the Alula Commissioner, E. Coronaro received orders in April 1924 to carry out a reconnaissance on the territories targetted for invasion. In spite of the forty year Italian relationship with the sultanates, Italy did not have adequate knowledge of the geography. During this time, the Stefanini-Puccioni geological survey was scheduled to take place, so it was a

---

8. Ibid., pp.152-153.

good opportunity for the expedition of Coronaro to join with this.[9]

Coronaro's survey concluded that the Majeerteen Sultanate depended on sea traffic, therefore, if this were blocked any resistance which could be mounted came after the invasion of the sultanate would be minimal.[10]

As the first stage of the invasion plan Governor De Vecchi ordered the two Sultanates to disarm. The reaction of both sultanates was to object, as they felt the policy was in breach of the protectorate agreements. The pressure engendered by the new development forced the two rival sultanates to settle their differences over Nugaal possession, and form a united front against their common enemy.

The First Casualty: Hobyo

The Sultanate of Hobyo was different from that of Majeerteen in terms of its geography and the pattern of the territory. It was founded by Yusuf Ali in the middle of the nineteenth century in central Somaliland. The jurisdiction of Hobyo stretched from El-Dheere through to Dusa-Mareeb in the south-west, from Galladi to Galkayo in the west, from Jerriiban to Garaad in the northeast, and the Indian Ocean in the east.[11]

By 1st October, De Vecchi's plan was to go into action. The operation to invade Hobyo started in October 1925. Columns of the new Zaptié began to move towards the sultanate. Hobyo, El-Buur, Galkayo, and the territory between were

---

9. Cesare Maria De Vecchi, *Orizzonti d'Impero*, 1935, p.76.
10. Ibid., p.111.
11. Ibid., pp.121-122.

completely overrun within a month. Hobyo was transformed from a sultanate into an administrative region. Sultan Yusuf Ali surrendered. Nevertheless, soon suspicions were aroused as Trivulzio, the Hobyo commissioner, reported movement of armed men towards the borders of the sultanate before the takeover and after.

Before the Italians could concentrate on the Majeerteen, they were diverted by new setbacks. On 9 November, the Italian fear was realised when a mutiny, led by one of the military chiefs of Sultan Ali Yusuf, Omar Samatar, recaptured El-Buur. Soon the rebellion expanded to the local population. The region went into revolt as El-Dheere also came under the control of Omar Samatar. The Italian forces tried to recapture El-Buur but they were repulsed. On 15 November the Italians retreated to Bud Bud and on the way they were ambushed and suffered heavy casualties.

While a third attempt was in the last stages of preparation, the operation commander, Lieutenant-Colonel Splendorelli, was ambushed between Bud Bud and Buula Barde. He and some of his staff were killed.[12]

As a consequence of the death of the commander of the operations and the effect of two failed operations intended to overcome the El-Buur mutiny, the spirit of Italian troops began to wane. The Governor took the situation seriously, and to prevent any more failure he requested two battalions from Eritrea to reinforce his troops, and assumed lead of the operations.[13] Meanwhile, the rebellion was gaining sympathy across the country, and as far afield as Western Somaliland.

---

12. Ibid., p.153.
13. Ibid., p.154.

The fascist government was surprised by the setback in Hobyo. The whole policy of conquest was collapsing under its nose. The El-Buur episode drastically changed the strategy of Italy as it revived memories of the Adowa fiasco when Italy had been defeated by Abyssinia. Furthermore, in the Colonial Ministry in Rome, senior officials distrusted the Governor's ability to deal with the matter. Rome instructed De Vecchi that he was to receive the reinforcement from Eritrea, but that the commander of the two battalions was to temporarily assume the military command of the operations and De Vecchi was to stay in Muqdisho and confine himself to other colonial matters. In the case of any military development, the military commander was to report directly to the Chief of Staff in Rome.[14]

While the situation remained perplexed, De Vecchi moved the deposed sultan to Muqdisho. Fascist Italy was poised to reconquer the sultanate by whatever means. To manoeuvre the situation within Hobyo, they even contemplated the idea of reinstating Ali Yusuf. However, the idea was dropped after they became pessimistic about the results.

To undermine the resistance, however, and before the Eritrean reinforcement could arrive, De Vecchi began to instill distrust among the local people by buying the loyalty of some of them. In fact, these tactics had better results than had the military campaign, and the resistance began gradually to wear down. Given the anarchy which would follow,[15] the new policy was a success.

---

14. Ibid., p.148.
15. Ibid., p.73.

On the military front, on 26 December 1925 Italian troops finally overran El-Buur, and the forces of Omar Samatar were compelled to retreat to Western Somaliland.

The Second Casuality: The Fall of the Majeerteen Sultanate

By neutralising Hobyo, the fascists could concentrate on the Majeerteen. In early October 1924, E. Coronaro, the new Alula commissioner, presented Boqor Osman with an ultimatum to disarm and surrender.

Meanwhile, Italian troops began to pour into the sultanate in anticipation of this operation. While landing at Haafuun and Alula, the sultanate's troops opened fire on them. Fierce fighting ensued and to avoid escalating the conflict and to press the fascist government to revoke their policy, Boqor Osman tried to open a dialogue. However, he failed, and again fighting broke out between the two parties.

Following this disturbance, on 7 October the Governor instructed Coronaro to order the Sultan to surrender; to intimidate the people he ordered the seizure of all merchant boats in the Alula area. At Haafuun, Arimondi bombarded and destroyed all the boats in the area.[16]

On 13 October Coronaro was to meet Boqor Osman at Baargaal to press for his surrender. Under siege already, Boqor Osman was playing for time. However, on 23 October Boqor Osman sent an angry response to the Governor defying his order. Following this a full scale attack was ordered in November. Baargaal was bombarded and razed to the ground.[17] This region was ethnically compact, and was out of range of

---

16. Ibid., p.126.
17. Ibid., pp.130-1.

direct action by the fascist government of Muqdisho. The attempt of the colonisers to suppress the region erupted into explosive confrontation.

The Italians were meeting fierce resistance on many fronts. In December 1925, led by the charismatic leader Hersi Boqor, son of Boqor Osman, the sultanate forces drove the Italians out of Hurdia and Haafuun, two strategic coastal towns on the Indian Ocean. Another contingent attacked and destroyed an Italian communications centre at Cape Guardafui, on the tip of the Horn. In retaliation Bernica and other warships were called on to bombard all main coastal towns of the Majeerteen. After a violent confrontation Italian forces captured Ayl (Eil), which until then had remained in the hands of Hersi Boqor.[18]

In response to the unyielding situation, Italy called for reinforcements from their other colonies, notably, Eritrea. With their arrival at the closing of 1926, the Italians began to move into the interior where they had not been able to venture since their first seizure of the coastal towns. Their attempt to capture Dharoor Valley was resisted, and ended in failure.

De Vecchi had to reassess his plans as he was being humiliated on many fronts. After one year of exerting full force he could not yet manage to gain a result over the sultanate.

In spite of the fact that the Italian navy sealed the sultanate's main coastal entrance, they could not succeed in stopping them from receiving arms and ammunition through it. It was only early 1927 when they finally succeeded in shutting

---

18. Robert L Hess, *Italian Colonialism in Somalia*, p.55.

the northern coast of the sultanate, thus cutting arms and ammunition supplies for the Majeerteen.

By this time, the balance had tilted to the Italian's side, and in January 1927 they began to attack with a massive force, capturing Iskushuban, at the heart of the Majeerteen. Hersi Boqor unsuccessfully attacked and challenged the Italians at Iskushuban. To demoralise the resistance, ships were ordered to raze and bombard the sultanate's coastal towns and villages.[19] In the interior the Italian troops confiscated livestock.

By the end of the 1927 the Italians had nearly taken control of the sultanate. Defeated and humiliated, Hersi Boqor and his top staff were forced to retreat to Ethiopia in order to rebuild the forces. However, they had an epidemic of cholera which frustrated all attempts to recover his force.

After two years of devastating war in which thousands of civilians died and the entire economy of the sultanate was ruined, razing all coastal towns and villages, the Italian colonial administration could boast that it had broken the Majeerteen resistance and put an end to an era in Somaliland.

Boqor Osman fled to the British Somaliland, but was handed back to the Italians. In November the formal act of surrender took place in Hurdia, and Boqor Osman dramatically consigned his sword to Governor De Vecchi.[20] Later Boqor Osman was exiled to Muqdisho.

With the elimination of the north-eastern sultanates and the breaking of the Benaadir resistance, from this period henceforth, Italian Somaliland was to become a reality.

---

19. Cesare Maria De Vecchi, *Orizzonti d'Impero*, pp.50-70.
20. Robert L Hess, *Italian Colonialism in Somalia*, 1966, p.156.

The partition of Somaliland was already shaping during this period and the fate of the Somalis was at the mercy of the colonial powers.

Chapter III

MODERN SOMALI NATIONALISM (1920-1960)

Somali nationalism began early with Ahmed Gurey (Ahmed Ibrahim al-Ghasi or Gran, left-handed) when he successfully pushed back the Christian Abyssinians to the Kaffa province at the end of the sixteenth century. Somali nationalism is not the result of the influence of western ideology, but springs from the very nature of Somali culture and is nurtured by a feeling of national consciousness which focuses on the shared heritage of Islam and belief in a common ancestor, both of which make for a strong sense of a pan-Somali cultural nationalism.[21] This nationalism was reawakened in the twentieth century as a result of external influence such as

---

21. Abdirahman Ali Hersi, *The Arab Factor in Somali History, op. cit.*, p.18-19.

the establishment of an alien government, the impact of the Second World War and news of the struggles for independence in other countries.[22]

As the Somalis had never been subjected to institutionalised government except under that of the authority of elders, they felt uneasy with the interruption of their traditional way of life by the colonialists.[23] Colonial rivalries and foreign interests in the Somali territory led to its being partitioned between Britain, Italy, France and Abyssinia (present Ethiopia).

The Somali reaction to alien domination was always aggressive and served to emphasise a Somali common identity.

Almost Under One Flag

In 1935, Italy with its locally constituted army, successfully invaded Abyssinia (Ethiopia) from its Somali territory. This invasion followed on from a series of incidents in the early 1930s, culminated in the Wal-waal (Wal Wal) incident in November 1934, in which Italy and Abyssinia were involved in disputes over thier respective interpretations of the 1897 agreement on a common border. With this latest conquest, Italy now controlled most of the Horn, from its Eritrean colony on the Red Sea, through Abyssinia to Somalia in the south; the exceptions were the two small territories of British Somaliland and French Somaliland.

In August 1940, now within the context of the Second World War, Italy invaded British Somaliland. The occupation was short lived, however, as the allied forces seized Muqdisho on 25 February 1941, and in March advanced to win back

---

22. Saadia Touval, *Somali Nationalism, op. cit.*, pp.83-84.
23. Ibid., pp.61-63.

British Somaliland. In 1941 all Somali territories (with the exception of French Somaliland which remained under the Vichy rule), were destined to remain under the British flag for nearly a decade.

The victorious allied forces divided the liberated area into British Somaliland, the former Italian Somaliland and Hawd (Haud) which lay south of British Somaliland. British Somaliland and Hawd (Haud) were to remain in the hands of the British. The fate of the former Italian Somaliland was that of the other Italian colonies of Eritrea, Libya and Cyrenaica.

Ernest Bevin, the then British Foreign Secretary, recommended that all Somali territories be put under one political union under trusteeship. He read his proposal to the House of Commons on 4 June 1946. In his speech Mr. Bevin said,

> ... In the latter part of the last century the Horn of Africa was divided between Great Britain, France and Italy. At about the time we occupied our part, the Ethiopians occupied an inland area which is the grazing ground for nearly half the nomads of British Somaliland, for six months of the year. Similarly, the nomads of Italian Somaliland must cross the existing frontiers in search of grass. In all innocence, therefore, we proposed that British Somaliland, Italian Somaliland, and the adjacent part of Ethiopia, if Ethiopia agreed, should be lumped together as a trust territory, so that the nomads should lead their frugal existence with the least possible hindrance and there might be a real chance of a decent economic life, as understood in that

territory. ... If the Conference does not like our proposal, we will not be dogmatic about it; we are prepared to see Italian Somaliland put under the United Nations' trusteeship.[24]

However, the plan, known as the Bevin Plan, was bitterly opposed by the USSR as well as the other allied powers, the USA and France, who were suspicious of the British proposal. Britain, as had been seen before, had tried to retain Western Somaliland as part of the Bevin Plan for Somali unification.

In the same year negotiations took place between Britain and Ethiopia 'in which the possible exchange of a part of British Somaliland and the Hawd was discussed, with a view to granting Ethiopia direct access to the sea, while permitting the British administration to remain permanently in charge of the territories in which Somali nomads from the British Somaliland grazed their livestock during part of each year'. However, as a result of the Federation of Ethiopia and Eritrea, the Ethiopians had added the coast of Eritrea to their territory, making further negotiating with Britain unnecessary.[25]

Nevertheless, Britain decided to surrender Western Somaliland to Ethiopia in fulfilment of the 1942 and 1944 Anglo-Ethiopian Agreements. It is against this background, that on 29 November 1954, an agreement was concluded between the governments of Great Britain and Ethiopia by which Great Britain transferred the valuable Hawd

---

24. Somali Republic, *The Somali Peninsula*, 1962.
25. Lathan Brown, D.J., The Ethiopia-Somaliland Frontier Dispute, (International and Comparative Law Quarterly), quoted in *The Somali Peninsula*, 1962, pp.70-71.

and Reserved Area[26] of Western Somaliland to Ethiopian administrative control. This transfer was greeted by the Somalis with an outburst of indignation. The agreement terminated the 1944 Agreement which provided for the continuation of the British Military Administration in the Hawd (Haud) and Reserved Areas without prejudice to Ethiopia's sovereignty.

The British Secretary of State for the Colonies in a statement to the House of Commons said in 1955 that he regretted the Treaty of 1897 `... but, like much that has happened before, it is impossible to undo it'.[27] The original Anglo-Somali Treaties of Protection did not cede any territory to Britain, as had apparently been recognised by the text of the 1897 treaty and annexation of Ethiopia, the British Government now evidently arrived at a new and different interpretation of the position. It was in this way that the Anglo-Ethiopian Agreement of 1954 purported to recognise the sovereignty of Ethiopia over Somali territory, to which she had no prior title.[28]

This agreement and the subsequent transfer were conducted in breach of the Anglo-Somali agreements and in the utmost secrecy without regard for universally accepted human rights, freedom of choice and the right to self-determination. This led to a breach of trust between the British and the Somali clans.

---

26. This region was part of Western Somaliland with the Ogaden and Hawd (Haud).
27. Somali Republic, *The Somali Peninsula, 1962, op. cit.*, pp.75-77.
28. Ibid., p.76.

Nationalism in the Italian Somaliland

The Somali abhorrence of Christian rule is based on their belief that Islam is superior to all other religions. The Euro-Christian occupation of their territory triggered anti-colonialist sentiment in all Somali territories.[29] Resistance to the colonial authority erupted sporadically in many places and in response, colonial powers dealt harshly with insurgency to impose their rule in the country.

Italy, which ruled Italian Somaliland, succeeded in establishing its authority only after repressive measures.[30] Nonetheless, it was only after they eliminated the north-eastern sultanates in 1927, and broke the Biyamaal and Wa'daan resistance in Benaadir at the end of 1908, that they could create what became known as Italian Somaliland.

A sizeable Italian population settled in the area between the two rivers, Jubba and Shabeelle, as farmers. These settlements needed manpower for their huge plantations. This created difficulties because waged work was alien to the local inhabitants. In order to recruit a work force, a law was passed which forced inhabitants of the region to work as labourers on the farms. More rigid systems were introduced by the fascist government in 1938 in which control of trade and commerce were to be taken over by government monopolies and para-statal organisations. The system excluded Somalis or colonial "subjects" in any sector of the economy where they might be in competition with Italians.[31] Despite the fascist policy of Italian colonialism, the foundation of a modern

---

29. Saadia Touval, *Somali Nationalism, op. cit.*, pp.61-63.
30. Ibid., p.71.
31. I M Lewis, *A Modern History of Somalia, op. cit.*, pp.110-12.

colony had been laid down in the Italian Somaliland. Differing from other Somali territories, public buildings, roads, and plantation industries were created. The economic activities in agricultural, commercial and industrial enterprises, launched by Italians, initiated a trend of social change. Despite the fact that everything was owned by Italians, Arabs and Asians, the Somalis were recruited as workers. The new economic life introduced a new lifestyle which in turn gave a new stimulus to modern Somali nationalism.[1]

The new economic activity in these parts attracted many people from rural and nomadic areas as it provided them with new experiences which were different from those lived by their fathers and forefathers. Many of then went into private enterprise as traders and merchants, while many others worked as clerks in the colonial offices. While still influenced by the clan system, the new urban élite was experiencing centralised authority under colonial rule. This promoted new social and political attitudes and modern schooling further accelerated these changes.

These urban areas of traders, merchants and the new élite, demanded a different sort of cooperation from the traditional system of the pastoral society. Further, western influence and the long suppressed reaction to alien rule provided conditions favourable to the emergence of new aspirations leading to the creation of a modern nationalist movement.

Parties in the Italian Somaliland

In March 1941 Britain took control of Somali territories from Italy. The Ogaadeen, the Reserved Area, the Hawd (all

---

1. Saadia Touval, *Somali Nationalism, op. cit.*, pp.72-3.

three in Western Somaliland), and Italian Somaliland were under British Military Administration based in Muqdisho, while British Somaliland had its own military governor. The British Military Administration had to reconstruct the territories' administrative system, which had broken down during the war with Italy. In 1946 it created the District and Provincial Advisory Councils which encouraged people's participation in their district affairs, and lifted the ban on political debates.[2] A few years before this period, nationalist organisations appeared, the first and most important of these being the Somali Youth Club founded on 15 May 1943 in Muqdisho. Representing the majority of the main Somali clan groups, the thirteen founding members were united in the desire to abolish the divisive elements in society and to establish a new conception of nationhood based on Islam as the unifying force married with the modern consciousness of nationhood by inculcating a code of loyalty transcending tribal and clan schism.[3]

In 1947 the club changed its name to the Somali Youth League (SYL) and reorganised and widened its goals and its main objectives as follows: (1) to unite all Somalis, (2) to educate youth in the modern ways of life, and (3) to adopt the Osmaniya (Osmania) Somali script. Osmania script was founded in 1920s and soon became the vehicle with which the leaders of modern Somali nationalists to champion as the "symbol of the Somali achievement."[4]

---

2. I M Lewis, *A Modern History of Somalia, op. cit.*, p.119.
3. Ibid., pp.122-123.
4. Ibid., pp.115-23. The script was founded by the linguist Cismaan Yuusuf Keenadiid.

While some parties had aims which transcended tribalism, there were others whose sole aim was their traditional interest, and one of these was the Independent Constitutional Party (Digil and Mirifle Party) known also as Hisbul Disturul Digil & Mirifle (HDSM), formed in March 1947. The HDSM represented the Digil and Mirifle clans of Italian Somaliland, namely the Rahanweyn, Digil, Bantu and some Arab communities. For the need to adjust to nationalist enthusiasm and to legalise as a party, the HSDM changed its denomination to Hisbul Dasturul Mustaqili Soomaali (HDSM) (later it became the second largest party in independent Somalia).

After the defeat of Italy in 1945, a commission consisting of Representatives of the Four Powers (Britain, USSR, US and France), was established to investigate the wishes of the former Italian Somaliland, concerning their political future. The other Somali territories were ignored.

The arrival of the commission in Muqdisho in January 1948 aroused frenetic political activities, sometimes resulting in bloody confrontations between opposing groups. Whatever the result, the new situation stimulated the environment and transformed nascent nationalistic parties into mass organizations.[5] The SYL's suggested programme was ten years of UN Trusteeship by the four powers, whereas the Hisbi Tasturi Mustaqilla proposed thirty years of UN Trusteeship under Italian control.

The commission granted every political party the opportunity to write its own manifesto and display to the public. On 11 January while SYL and its supporters were

---

5. Saadia Touval, *Somali Nationalism, op. cit.*, p.81.

rallying, the Italian community and their supporters tried to interfere. Fighting erupted between the two groups and in the event 15 Somalis and 51 Italians died.

Later, the commission reported to the UN that the SYL represented the wish of most of the Somali people. And in November 1949, the UN appointed Italy to administer the Somali territory for ten years under the United Nations mandate. Accordingly, in February 1956 the first Legislative Assembly of 99 members was formed and selected Abdullahi Isse as Prime Minister.

While Italian Somaliland was on track for independence, the SYL leadership broke up after its president, Haji Mahamed Husein, was expelled from the party in April 1958. Haji Mahamed Husein was critical of the Prime Minster and the President of the Assembly, Adan Abdulle Osman, for what he called "their weak stand on pan-Somali unity".[6] Angered by the expulsion, Haji Mahamed Husein and his supporters formed the Greater Somali League (Gereedka) in the following year.

Parties in British Somaliland

In British Somaliland the strong feeling of nationalism had been aroused by the small overseas Somali community, mainly in Aden who formed the Somali Islamic Association, when the Somaliland National Society was emerging in the British Somaliland in 1945. After a few years, the SNS merged with other political associations which had been active since 1935. In 1951 it reorganised itself and assumed a new name, the Somali National League (SNL) and it set

---

6. I M Lewis, *A Modern History of Somalia, op. cit.*, pp. 157-58.

its own political programmes as following, (i) independence and unification of the Somali people under one political unit, (ii) social, political and economic development, and (iii) the cessation of tribal feuding.

An educated élite began to develop in British Somaliland in the inter-war period. Before the introduction of western education in British Somaliland, only Qoranic schools existed in the country. The French catholic mission, which was established in 1891, was closed down by the British authority because of pressure from the Muslim religious authority. The religious leaders feared the missionary schools might be used as an instrument for Christianising children. In fact, as a result of this fear bloody resistance culminated in riots in Bur-o' in 1922 and 1939. As British interest in the territory was only strategic and logistic, they used the religious leaders' objection as a pretext to ignore the country's educational development.[7]

After the defeat of Italy in 1941, Britain gained control of British Somaliland which she had lost to Italy in 1939. She also gained dominion of Italian Somaliland, the Ogaadeen and Hawd (the last two being part of Western Somaliland). The negotiations for the future of Italian Somaliland greatly affected the people in British Somaliland.

Due to geographical proximity, the nationalist ideas propagating in Asia and the Middle East spread. During the same period, Britain decided to cede Hawd to the Ethiopia and this provoked a widespread outcry with massive

---

7. Maxamed D. Afrax, "The Mirror of Culture", : Somali Dissolution Seen Through Oral Expression" in *The Somali Challenge*, ed. Ahmed I. Samatar, 1994, pp. 233-249.

demonstrations throughout British Somaliland, Western Somaliland (the Ogaadeen, the Reserved Area, the Hawd) and Italian Somaliland. Political awakening spread rapidly via the nomads where before interest in politics had been confined to the educated élite.[8] The protest prompted the reawakening from lethargy of the Somali political consciousness. And the nationalistic political parties found fertile ground in this new wave of political protest gaining sympathy in British Somaliland, Italian Somaliland, and in other parts Somali territory.

The nomadic people of British and Italian Somalilands depended on the Hawd, which is rich in grazing ground for their livelihood. The Hawd, as part of the Reserved Area, remained under British Administration until a new Anglo-Ethiopian agreement was concluded on 26 November 1954.

The new political situation created a new political convention, the National United Front (NUF), which in 1955 began to press the British to reverse the decision of relinquishing the Hawd (Haud) to Ethiopia. The NUF provided a political framework for cooperation for many political parties, among them SYL, SNL and other organisations like the Somali Officials' Union, which represented the civil service. However, the convention was short lived as SYL and SNL withdrew from it. Later NUF evolve into a political party.

These new circumstances forced the British Administration to introduce limited political autonomy in the territory by establishing, in 1947, an Advisory Council which was appointed on a tribal basis. The council's purpose was to stimulate the interest of the people in the administration

---

8. I M Lewis, rev. ed. *A Modern History of Somalia, op.cit*, pp.160-80.

of the territory, and to collect public funds. In 1951, the administration introduced the District Advisory Council. The Local Authority Ordinance, which was enacted in 195,0 gave limited judicial powers to *Aqils (or Akhil).*[9]

Similarly, in March 1959, the first election was held followed by a second one in the following February in which the leader of the SNL, Mahamed Haji Ibrahim Igal, was called to be the Leader of Government Business in the Legislature on 6 April 1960.

The new Legislative Council passed a resolution calling for independence and union with Italian Somaliland when the latter gained its independence on 1 July 1960. In reply to the resolution, Alan Lennox-Boyd, the then British Colonial Secretary, declared that Britain had no objection to the union of the British Somaliland with Italian Somaliland.

To ease the aspirations of the people of the two territories, the National Pan-Somali Movement had been formed in Muqdisho in 1959. Delegates from all Somali territories participated in the conference. The new movement aimed at uniting the territories.

The Western Somaliland Political Activities[10]

It is not possible to describe the effect of imperial partition of Somali territories in the closing decades of the nineteenth

---

9. I M Lewis, *A Pastoral Democracy, op. cit*, pp.30-90.
10. Western Somaliland, generally known as Ogaadeen, is in the eastern part of Ethiopia. It is exclusively inhabited by ethnic Somalis. The territory comprised the Ogaadeen, Hawd (Reserved Area was part of Hawd). The Ogaadeen clan (Daarood) form the majority of the Somali clans inhabitant in this territory.

century without mentioning Ethiopian participation. In fact, the roots of the present turmoil in the Horn of Africa go back to this period when a triumphant Ethiopian prince, Menelik II, took advantage of a number of propitious events and extended Ethiopian authority in territory inhabited by the Somalis and Oromo.[11]

Whilst in British and Italian Somaliland the majority of the population were fighting for independence, in Western Somaliland Somalis were fighting against the surrender of their territory to Ethiopia by the British government. As early as 1942 there had been disturbances in the Jigjiga region caused by Ethiopia's attempt to impose direct taxation on Somalis. Two years later, Somalis petitioned the British Military Administration, urging it not to transfer Western Somaliland territory to Ethiopian control.

Surprisingly, after the Second World War, Britain had a change of heart and proposed that the interests of the Somali people would be best served if all the Somali territories were united under a single administration. Nonetheless, the plan known as the Bevin Plan, was rejected by the other victorious powers of the Second World War, the USA, USSR and France. Ironically, while on one hand Britain was suggesting the idea to put all Somalis under one political authority, she was also making secret deals with Ethiopia to transfer control of the Somali territory to Ethiopian administration. During the process of transfer, the inhabitants of the region were never at any stage consulted or informed of the fact that their territory would be transferred to their traditional

---

11. Said S. Samatar and David D. Laitan, *Somalia: Nation in Search of a State*, op. cit. p.123.

enemy, Ethiopia. The British authorities took that course of action despite their knowledge that Somalis had occupied these lands for centuries, and the fact that the overwhelming majority of the Somalis had strong historical reasons for not wishing to be associated with Ethiopia. Britain was betraying the Somalis, as they were breaching the Anglo-Somali treaties of 1884-1885.[12]

When the Somalis realised what had happened, they were outraged by the agreement and the betrayal by Britain which had "pledged never to cede, sell, mortgage or otherwise give for occupation save the British Government, any portion of the territory presently inhabited by them or being under their control."[13]

Furthermore, the unification and independence of the two territories, the Italian and British Somalilands, in July 1960, raised much reaction in all Somali territories still under domination. In protest of still being under domination, in many Western Somaliland towns people were outraged and many Somali governors resigned. And in reaction, on 16 June 1963 the Western Somali Liberation Front (WSLF) was born. Garaad Makhtal Garaad Dahir became its first president. With the help from the Somali Republic, the WSLF started an armed struggle in the Western Somaliland. The Prime Minister of the Republic, Dr Abdirashid Ali Sharmaarke, gave public support materially and morally to the WSLF. Following the escalation of hostility, relationships between

---

12. Louis Fitzgibbon, *The Betrayal of the Somalis*, 1982, p.15.
13. Ibid, pp. 15-20.

Somalia and Ethiopia soured and hostilities grew to armed clashes in October 1963 and in February 1964.[14]

The French Somaliland's Political Activities

As France's need to occupy the Horn was commercial and centred on the need for a refuelling station to supply their ships to the Far East, Djibouti, in the French Somaliland, developed to become one of the busiest ports in the Horn before the Second World War.

In early 1931 the Somalis formed the Seamen's Union, an organisation which was concerned with port activities, and the political and economic affairs of the Somalis.[15] In 1945, the Territorial Council was formed from which the *loi cadre* in 1957 established an elected legislature responsible for internal affairs. The first election was won by the Union Republican, a coalition party representing the Somali, Afar and Arab population. Mahamud Harbi, leader of the Union Democaratique Somalie, became the Vice-President under the Governor who was the President of the colony.

The wind of Somali nationalism which blew from both British Somaliland and Italian Somaliland was felt in French Somaliland. To counter the tide, the Gaullists held a referendum to choose "independence or to remain as a French colony".

Mahamud Harbi campaigned for independence and union with Italian and British Somalilands when they attained

---

14. Mahamed-Abdi Mahamed, Autopsie de la crise, *in Forum: La guerre civile en Somalie: Quand? Comment? Pourquoi?* 7 et 8 Avril 1992, p.14.
15. Saadia Touval, *Somali Nationalism, op. cit.*, p.70.

their independence. Opposed to him was Hassan Guled who wished the territory to remain under France. Nonetheless, in strange and rather confusing circumstances, the territory's population voted against independence and preferred to remain an overseas territory of France. On 23 November 1958, a new election was held and Hassan Guled replaced Mahamud Harbi as Vice-President. Mahamud Harbi, defeated and humiliated, fled to Cairo, and later to Muqdisho in 1959, where he took part in the formation of the National Pan-Somali Conference.

In the aftermath of the referendum, the political situation started to deteriorate as the Issa Somalis (Ise) and Afar[16] populations began to vie for control of the territory. At the start of 1959 the Issa Somalis (Ise) were the largest block in the Territorial Assembly holding 14 out of 32 seats.[17] The political current was running in favour of the Afar as Ahmed Dini, an Afar, replaced Hassan Guled in April 1959.

Purged by his own group, in June 1960, Ahmed Dini was replaced by another Afar kinsman, Ali Arif Burhan.[18] In this period Somali political activity was in full tempo because of the Somali nationalistic fervour and, as a result, many of their leaders were compelled to go into exile. Their view of pan-Somalism openly collided with the French interests in the territory. By this time a clear division was eventually surfacing

---

16. In this part there are two ethnic groups: the Issa Somalis, who form the majority of the population, and the Afar. Somalis and Afar both form part of the Eastern Cushitic family of the Horn of Africa.
17. Saadia Touval, *Somali Nationalism, op. cit.*, pp.70-74.
18. Saadia Touval, *Somali Nationalism, op. cit.*, p.127.

in the political interests of the two main communities.[19] The French government took new measures to promote the Afar community, intending to drive a wedge between the two communities. The Afar, who were the most favoured, pushed France to change French Somaliland's name to the French Territory of the Afars and Ises.

The tension heightened when, in August 1966, Charles de Gaulle, while on a visit to Djibouti, was greeted by demonstrations for independence and anti-colonial slogans. And in reaction he announce a referendum in which the people could express "in a democratic way" their wish to remain (or not) as "a part of France". Simultaneously, the French government took drastic measures to deal with the independence activities. The French Legionnaires were dispatched to subdue the demonstrations.[20] Many died in the operation. More than five thousand people were arrested and nearly ten thousand were expelled. The expelled had been arrested by the French colonial authority and had their identity papers confiscated.[21]

The referendum took place on 19 March 1967, without the supervision of the United Nations, the Organisation of African Unity or any other international observer. Clearly, it was solely intended to maintain Djibouti's colonial status. The outcome, as announced by the French authority, was

---

19. Maryan Cumar Cali and Lidwien Kapteinjins, Cry for Independence, *Hal-Abuur*, Vol.1, Nos.2&3, Autumn/Winter 1993/1994, pp.26-7.
20. Ibid., pp.26-7.
21. Mahamed-Abdi Mahamed, Autopsie de la crise, in *Forum: La guerre civile en Somalie: Quand? Comment? Pourquoi?* 7 et 8 Avril 1992, p.19.

that 60% of the inhabitants of French Somaliland voted to remain as "part of France". Consequently, rioting broke out, and again the security forces had justification to suppress the riots with bloody methods.

The Northern Frontier District (NFD)

The Northern Frontier District (now known as North-Eastern Province of Kenya) comprised three separate administrative districts: Wajir, Garisa and Mandera. Somalis inhabit almost the whole of the eastern part of the region. Marked by the Somali line which ran southwards from the east of Moyale to the Tana River, the demarcation was created by the British administration to separate the Somali pastoral nomads from their ethnic kinsmen, the Orma and Borana.[1]

Until the 1940s, the NFD was isolated from the influence of the modern economy. Despite the pan-Somali wave which reached these parts at the end of the 1940s, political activities remained dormant until the 1960s when the British administration lifted a ban on political organization.[2] In this new situation, the Somalis could express their willingness and determination to join their kinsmen in the Somali Republic. Consequently new political parties emerged such as the Northern Province Peoples's Progressive Party (NPPPP), the Northern Frontier Democratic Party (NFDP) and the Northern Province Peoples' National Union (NPPNU). With the change in British attitude, the Somali leaders became optimistic about British acceptance of the will of its subjects.

---

1. I M Lewis, *A Modern History of Somalia, op. cit.*, pp.183-84.
2. Ibid., p.184.

Following developments in the same period in French Somaliland, (by this time French Territory of the Afar and Ises) and in Western Somaliland, the Somali government passed a motion in the National Assembly in November 1961 welcoming the union of the Northern Frontier District to the Republic. The political momentum in the region received new momentum with the motion. In the following year, at the Kenya Conference held in Lancaster House in London, the NFD delegation firmly voiced their desire to be granted an autonomous region that would eventually help union with the Somali Republic.[3] However, their request was sharply opposed by the Kenya African National Union (KANU) and the Kenya African Democratic Union (KADU) delegations. Paradoxically, while the KANU and KADU leaders were advocating their right of self-determination, they were deliberately opposing the same principles in the case of the Somalis. To ease the tension, the British Colonial Secretary at the time, Reginald Maulding, announced the appointment of a commission to survey the opinion of the people concerned.[4]

Meanwhile, the Somali government anxiously watched the course of events, and warned the British not to repeat past mistakes. The commission's findings based on a survey held in October 1962, were that the majority of the population favoured joining the Somali Republic.[5] However, the British

---

3. Mohammed I. Farah, *From Ethnic Response to Clan Identity*, op. cit., p.78.
4. Ibid., p.78.
5. Mahamed-Abdi Mahamed, Autopsie de la crise, in Forum: La guerre civile en Somalie: Quand? Comment? Pourquoi? 7 et 8 Avril

government did not honour its last undertakings given at the Kenya Conference in Lancaster House, but instead again betrayed the will of its subjects by announcing in early March 1963, that the NFD was to be brought into Kenya's regional constitution. The British decision led to general discontent throughout the NFD. Consequently, on 11 March 1963, the Somali Republic broke off diplomatic ties with Britain.

The British decision reflected favouritism towards Ethiopian imperialist policy and a desire not to endanger its relations with the new commonwealth country of Kenya. Had Somalia entered the Commonwealth states after its independence, perhaps the matter would not have ended in such a way.[6] Britain concentrated more on its future relations than on honouring its commitments and responsibilities over its subjects.

On 12 December 1963 Kenya received its independence. And in December 1965 President Julius Nyerere of Tanzania tried to open a dialogue between Kenya and Somalia in Arusha, but the rift between the two nations impeded all means of resolving the issue and led instead to their diplomatic rupture on 21 June 1966. To tighten its internal security, the Kenyan government took drastic security measures and ordered that whoever was to be found sympathetic to the *shifta*, the name given to the NFD Liberation Front activists, should be imprisoned for life and his property confiscated.[7]

1992, p.15. See also I M Lewis, *A Modern History of Somalia, op. cit.*, p.191.
6. I M Lewis, *A Modern History of Somalia, op. cit.*, p.195.
7. Mohammed I. Farah, *From Ethnic Response to Clan Identity, op. cit.*, pp.88-90.

Pan-Somalism

The Somali Republic's policy of uniting her remaining kinsmen under one flag had isolated it from the pan-African policy. By making pan-Somalis the driving force of their foreign policy, Somali nationalists regarded the principle of this policy as a wider application of the principles of pan-African unity, as it aimed at a legitimate unification of territories which colonialists' interests had arbitrarily destroyed. The policy of severing ethnic, cultural and economic links of the same people resulted in the Balkanization of Africa.

The Somali view was based on the assumption of cultural identity that ran counter to the process of national unification in other post-colonial African states constructed from widely different ethnic groups.[8] As Lewis reiterates, Their nationalism was tailor-made, and their problem was not that of nation-building, but of extending statehood outside the frontiers of the Somali Republic to embrace the remaining portions of the nation.[9]

---

8. I M Lewis, *A Modern History of Somalia, op. cit.*, p.196.
9. I M Lewis, *The Birth and Death of the Somali State*, p.1.

Chapter IV

COLONIAL LEGACY

European colonial intrusion at the end of the nineteenth century traumatised Somali society. It disrupted the harmony of a homogeneous group of people and eventually led to the partition of their territory into five different political entities. The legacy of the colonial partition of the Somali people is the root problem of the Horn of Africa. Somali nationalist aspirations and the intransigence of Somalia's neighbouring countries in not seeking to solve the territorial disputes provoked many international problems. For the Somali people the creation of an independent Somali Republic, on 1 July 1960, was only the beginning of their struggle for national unity. This linked those Somalis formerly ruled by Italian and British colonial powers. It excluded those living in

Ethiopia and Kenya, and Djibouti[10] that won independence from France only in June 1977.

The establishment of the Somali Republic was viewed by many nationalists as a step towards the culmination and realization of the Somali nation. Since independence in the 1960s almost all Somali foreign policy has focused on the task of putting all Somalis under a single state. This fact constituted 'a dilemma where Somalia remains a nation in search of a state'.[11] The idea of the 'unification of all Somalis' became the core of Somali aspirations.

The Country

The Somali Republic is bounded by the Indian Ocean to the east, the Gulf of Aden and the Red Sea to the north, by Ethiopia to the west and north-west, by Kenya to the southwest, and by the Republic of Djibouti to the northwest corner.

Along its northern coastline, which stretches for 2000 miles — the longest on the African continent — there is an extremely hot and arid coastal plain varying in width from some 70 miles on the west to a few feet on the east. This plain gives way to partly wooded mountains rising in the east to over 6000 feet. Beyond them is a vast tree-dotted

---

10. Roland Oliver and Michael Crowder, eds.; *The Cambridge Encyclopedia, op. cit.,* p.250.
11. Said Samatar and David Laitan, *Somalia: Nation in Search of a State, op. cit.,* p.129.

savannah of varying desiccation and fertility sloping gently down to the south.[12]

This abundant seasonal grazing land for Somali herds of livestock supports an immense number of fauna at all times. A large part of this vast inland plateau, which is the mainstream of life in the northern part of the country, lies beyond the *de facto* administrative borderline between Ethiopia and Somalia, and is bounded on the west by the remote Ethiopian highlands. Most areas of the expansive Somali country are intersected by an immense system of dry water courses or 'tugs', which flow during the rainy seasons.

The republic has two permanent flowing rivers, Jubba and Shabeelle, both of which rise in the Ethiopian highlands. The first meanders its way into the sea near Kismaayo in the extreme southern part of the country. The Shabeelle loses itself in marshes and sand dunes at Haway, a few miles inland and south of the ancient city of Barawa in southern Somalia.

Territorial Dispute

Under the Anglo-Ethiopian Agreements of 1942 and 1944, Britain relinquished Ogaadeen and Hawd,[13] (in Western Somaliland), to Ethiopia.

The territory that Somalia claimed in Ethiopia is sizeable, amounting to one fifth of Ethiopia's whole. She also claimed the Northern Frontier District (NFD), now known as the North-Eastern Province of Kenya.

---

12. Ministry of Information and National Guidance, *Somalia Today*, Somali Democratic Republic, Mogadishu, October 1970.
13. Hawd (Haud) lies east of Ogaden and was the last Somali territory relinquished by the British to the Ethiopian in 1954..

A large number of the Somali people remained outside the boundaries handed over to Somalia by the colonial powers. Samatar and Laitin describe the situation in this way:

> The most unfortunate consequence of Somali history for current politics is the fact that a significant percentage of those who are part of the Somali tradition do not live within the boundaries handed to Somalis by the colonial powers. Many of them still live as second class citizens in Kenya and as unwanted subjects in Ethiopia. Many straddle the borders and rely on water holes and grassland on both sides. This difficult situation has added to the pathos of the story of contemporary Somali politics [because of] the significance of this issue of boundaries, and a deep desire of so many Somalis to be united under the flag of a single state.[14]

In the 1940s a dispute over the border between the UN's Italian Trusteeship of Somalia and Ethiopia prompted the United Nations to advise Italy and Ethiopia to settle their differences. But Ethiopia, which had already acquired the Ogaadeen and Hawd through Anglo-Ethiopian agreements, was determined to push its border even further into Somali territory. It maintained that the frontier ran to the east near the coast. On the contrary, Italy claimed that the frontier lay to the west of the provisional line.[15] To advise on the matter, the UN appointed an arbitration tribunal led by Mr Trygve Lie, a former UN Secretary-General. The matter could not

---

14. Said S. Samatar and David Laitan, *Somalia: Nation in Search of a State*, op. cit., p.xvii.
15. I M Lewis, *A Modern History of Somalia*, op. cit., p.182.

be concluded because of Ethiopian intransigence. However, in December 1959 Ethiopia and Somalia (under the UN Trusteeship) agreed that until a final settlement could be reached, the British provisional line should remain in force. When in 1960 Somalia gained its independence the territorial dispute was still pending.

The Problem of Colonial Boundaries for Independent Africa

In the late 1950s and early 1960s it was believed that the boundaries of the newly emerging countries in Africa would generate many bitter conflicts. The boundary lines had been drawn by the colonial powers, and were seen to be unrealistic and unjust. Changing them would pose a serious threat to the existence of some states. The Organisation of African Unity (OAU), established in 1963 in Cairo as a regional body, aimed to address many pressing African issues including disputed boundaries. Instead, the OAU complicated the whole issue by accepting that all borders should remain as they were when the colonial powers left Africa. Somalia stood out in rejecting the OAU position that approved colonial borders.

Many African states were vulnerable and suspicious of any challenge to the colonially defined boundaries for fear that the framework of political entities in the continent might be swept away in an anarchy of tribal and other conflicts.[16]

The newly independent African states felt unable to tackle the disorder of land and people that the colonialists had left behind. For the Somalis, however, it represented the legitimisation of one African state colonising another. This

---

16. Alfred Gobban, *National Self-determination*, op. cit., 1945, P.31.

was a life and death matter for the Somalis. Acceptance of it could limit the movement of pastoralists to and from Western Somaliland. Western Somaliland is rich in pasture in the rainy seasons - April to June and October to November - and animals do not need much water as they get moisture from the green leaves. However, in the dry season the pastoralists would migrate with their animals to eastern Somalia where water is more abundant. Curbing their movements leaves the pastoralists vulnerable, as this pattern of movement is the time tested traditional response to drought.[17] The longer term consequence for the environment is deforestation and desertification, the result of over grazing. In the words of Louis Fitzgibbon,

> The Ogaadeen is a featureless expanse of desert and scrub. But to the Somali nomad pastoralists it is 'home', notwithstanding its meagre resources with respect to water and grazing. Its security was promised by the British colonialists after the 'scramble for Africa'. Yet it was they who, between 1890 and 1954 gave it away, piece by piece, to Abyssinia, the traditional enemy of the Somalis. It was that betrayal that has led to a century of suffering and strife, as well as death, and the time has now come when those who wish to retain their homeland can have a say with regard to its disposal.[18]

---

17. Philip Raikes, Food Shortages and Famine, in Society & Social Science: A Reader, ed. James Anderson et al., 1990, p.31.
18. Louis Fitzgibbon's remark to "The Ogaden Conflict 1977-1978" documentary video.

THE CIVILIAN GOVERNMENT (1960-1969)

The preamble of the Constitution of the Somali Republic promulgated in June 1961, stressed that Somalia become a unitary republic with a representative democratic form of government. The legislature was uni-cameral and composed of deputies elected by universal direct and secret suffrage for a term of five years and representing the whole people.[19] The first meeting of the National Assembly elected Adan Abdulle Osman, who had been for one year the provisional President. President Adan Abdulle Osman called Dr Abdirashid Ali Sharmaarke to form a government. After presenting his cabinet of 13 ministers to the National Assembly on 23 July, the new prime minister and his government prepared to face the most immediate problems facing the new state. Administratively the country was divided into eight regions and 47 districts each headed by a regional governor or district commissioner appointed by the Minister of the Interior.[20]

The newly formed state's first task was to break the colonial legacy and influence under which British and Italian Somalilands had developed during the colonial time.[21] The foremost difficulty was administrative and the matter was somewhat aggravated by linguistic barriers, as there was no official Somali script to facilitate the communication within the government. In the south, the Italian language was the

---

19. *Constitution of Somalia,* Fourth Part: Organisation of the State, Article 51, Mogadiscio, July 1, 1962, pp.786-787.
20. Irvin Kaplan...[and others], *Area Handbook for Somalia: Political,* 1969, pp.187-8.
21. Ibid., p.166.

main means of administrative and legal communication, and in the north English was mainly used.

The legal system in the southern region was based on customary and Islamic laws. However, in the northern region there was a different system based on the English common and statutory law, upon the Indian Penal code and Somali custom. To solve the legal problem, a unified legal system was introduced. The Supreme Court was instructed to establish two separate sections to deal with cases from the two regions.

Some difficulties were surmountable but others were more sensitive, such as that of tariff levels. To standardise the system, the tax rates of the northern region had to be raised to the levels of the southern region. The increases raised the price of essential commodities in the north. The exodus of the British expatriates also affected the northern economy causing economic decline in the region. Soon widespread discontent surfaced in the northern region, and people expressed their grievance in a referendum on the constitution of 1961, with 54,284 voting against and 49,527 for, whereas in the southern regions only 128,627 voted against and 1,711,013 voted in favour.[22]

The matter did not end there. After only a few months, in December 1961 a secessionist military coup was attempted led by twelve northern officers.[23] The objective was to detach the northern region from the Somali Republic. The revolt leaders were arrested by their subordinates who defied the orders of their own commanders. The plotters of the abortive

---

22. Saadia Touval, *Somali Nationalism, op. cit.*, p.121.
23. Preston King, *An African Winter*; 1986, p.123..

rebellion were pardoned in 1964 by the then President, Adan Abdulle Osman.

The new Republic inherited less than 200 kilometres of tarmac road, which ran from Muqdisho south to Marka and north to Jowhar.[24] In the rainy season the capital sometimes lost communication with the rest of the country, and had to rely on police long wave radios. The abortive coup drew attention to the need for improved communication between Hargeysa and Muqdisho. It also underlined the need for the government to speed up the achievement of administrative and other integrational processes.

Somalia in a State of War

The Somali intransigence on the question of its missing territories was creating more enemies than friends. A conference held in Lagos in January 1962 placed the Somali dispute before a commission purposely set up to deal with conflict between African states. However, at the Organisation of African Unity's summit in May 1963 in Addis Ababa, Haile Selassie played deft diplomatic games against Somalia on the issue of no border changes. He scored a notable tactical victory by further isolating Somalia. Despite African leaders knowing about the participation of Ethiopia in the scramble for Africa, they preferred to ignore Ethiopia's past roles.

By the end of 1963 the Somali leadership was weary of trying to find a diplomatic solution to their territorial claims.

---

24. Musollini's plan to create an Italian East African Empire involved a road which connected Ethiopia and Somalia. However, at the time of independence this road, which reached up to Feerfeer, Ethiopia, was out of use.

At home it faced growing opposition because of its lack of achievement.

The failure to realise concrete results through diplomacy, and the knowledge of the victimisation and marginalisation facing ethnic Somalis in Ethiopia, Kenya and French Somaliland contributed to the hostile attitude towards western countries. In fact, in November 1963, the Prime Minister, Dr Sharmaarke, announced the Republic's refusal of western military assistance in favour of Russian military aid amounting to nearly $22m. During the following years the Soviet Union payed increased attention to building the Somali army. The era of the Somali military buildup started in this period, and was later to intensify with the involvement of superpower rivalry in the Horn. The resources and energy needed for national development had been channelled into securing the liberation of the Somalis still under colonial rule. This policy resulted in making enemies of its neighbours, Ethiopia and Kenya, and many other potential friends. Somalia was seen as a state at war with others.

In September 1964 President Adan Abdulle Osman dismissed Dr Sharmaarke and called Abdirisaq Haji Husein to form a new government. Premier Abdirisaq Haji Husein had a pro-western tendency and President Adan Abdulle Osman chose him in an attempt to improve relations with the West. However, the new premier did not change the Government's stance towards Ethiopia, Kenya and France.

At home, Premier Abdirisaq Haji Husein introduced bold reforms in government administration by mounting an anticorruption campaign against incompetent government bureaucracy. The campaign was known as *busta rosso* (the red envelope) named after the official envelope received by those bureaucrats who were going to be fired. These new drives had created many enemies by the time of the presidential election. On 10 June 1967, President Adan Abdulle Osman's six year term of office expired, and he lost to Dr Abdirashid Ali Sharmaarke.

On 20 July 1967, the new president appointed Mahamed Haji Ibrahim Igal as premier. Rejecting the fruitless external policy of his predecessor, Premier Mahamed Haji Ibrahim Igal took daring political initiatives. He changed the aggressive political tone towards Somalia's neighbours to a more conciliatory one. He met Kenyan and Ethiopian leaders at the October 1967 OAU meeting in Arusha, Tanzania, and exchanged positive views. He agreed upon normalisation of relations, and the opening of negotiations through the good office of President Kenneth Kaunda of Zambia. At the end of 1967, he reestablished diplomatic relations with Britain. He also declared that Djibouti belonged to France and that the Djiboutians must negotiate with France for their independence.

Instead, the new political drive of Premier Mahamed Haji Ibrahim Igal met stiff resistance at home. He was seen as drifting out of the Republic's foreign policy mainstream by normalizing relations with the 'enemies' of the Somali nation. He was accused of a 'sell out', and his government grew more unpopular as the time for parliamentary elections approached.

The Failure of the Civilian Government

The new classes of political leaders gallantly tried to set up democratic practices, but they were incapable of mustering their energy to generate economic and social change.[1]

A few benefits however, were enjoyed by the people, such as freedom of speech, of association, of assembly and of the press. For example *Dalka*, a monthly newspaper published in English, *Tribuna*, another monthly newspaper in Italian, and several Arabic weekly newspapers were often critics of the government. There was an independent judiciary where cases were tried by qualified judges, men of integrity and experience independent of interference or dictation from other organ of the state. There was also a multi-party system where issues were openly aired at public meetings.[2] Nevertheless, the fact was that the civilian government lacked any serious commitment to development, as they were guilty of glaring neglect for the needs of economic and social progress. Somalia was experiencing all kinds of democracy's ailments, and the deepening of corruption and the incompetence of the civilian government were deflating any democratic benefit. Party politics had fallen short of what the Somali people were expecting from the exercise of democracy. The democratic parliamentary process that was 'expected' to go well with the traditional political institutions turned sour.[3] Like in

---

1. Hassan Ali Mirreh, "Providing for the Future: Memory, Mutuality and Obligation", in *The Somali Challenge: Peace, Resources and Reconstruction*, Geneva, 10-14 July 1992
2. Ibid., p.6
3. Ali Mazrui and Michael Tidy, *Nationalism and New States of Africa*, 1984, p.20.

many African countries, there was misuse of the European models of government. Emphasis was on party politics and personal power rather than on mobilization for national development.[4] Corruption became rife and deputies traded their votes for personal gain. Sixty-four parties with 1000 candidates took part in the March 1969 election.[5] The system facilitated anarchy, as the poet Nuur Ali Qonof warned in the following verse[6] a few months prior to the military takeover in October 1969:

> The much aspired to state has faltered,
> Charlatans and impostors have ravaged the essence of parliament,
> Lost are the guiding Constitution and sense of direction.
> Since the leading demons are devoid of care, Nor will there be a new moon or a saviour,
> Incoherent are the objectives and aspirations of the

---

4. Ibid., p.22.
5. S. Samatar and D. Laitan, *Somalia: Nation in Search of a State*, op. cit., p.76.
6. The Somali version of the poem *La Hubsandoone* by Xirsi Cali Qonof:
    Habbis baa ku dhacay dowladdii lagu han weynaaye
    How-howlayaal soo geliyo heeran baa dilaye
    Dastuur lagu hagaagiyo la waa hilin la qaadaaye.
    Kolna haddaan dujaalada hurriyo hoosta dhuganayne
    Ama aan hilaal noo dhashiyo haadi imanaynin
    Kala maqan hawada Leegadiyo himiladoodiye
    Inqilaab hurdada uu ku jiro la hubsandoonee.

Leego,[7] The continued lying in wait of a *coup d'état* will be seen.

Before a solution to the languishing democracy could be found, the situation took a new turn when, on Wednesday 15 October 1969 during a tour, the President was assassinated in Las Anod by a member of his own police force. Although said to be personally and not politically motivated, the incident created a political vacuum and exacerbated the tense and unstable political atmosphere.[8] The situation was taken advantage of by the army, which seized power on Tuesday 21 October at 03.00 a.m. in a 'bloodless coup'.

The takeover was widely welcomed and was seen as giving relief from the political and social tension built up by the party system. The perception that the army saved the country from plunging into chaos enhanced the prestige of the military force known as *Xoogga Dalka* (literally, the power of the country).

The military *junta* rounded up all civil government members including members of the previous civil administration, the former president Adan Abdulle Osman, the former prime ministers, Abdirisaq Haji Husein and Mahamed Haji Ibrahim Igal, and the former Police Commander General Mahamed Abshir Muse. They were accused of corruption and embezzlement of government funds. Subsequently, they were to remain imprisoned for many years without trial.

---

7. Leego is the Somali Youth League party which led Somalia to independent.
8. An African Watch Report, Somalia: A Government at War with its Own People, January 1990, p.14.

The military *junta* suspended the Constitution and the Supreme Court, closed the National Assembly and barred all political parties.[9] It announced the establishment of a Supreme Revolutionary Council (SRC) on 1 November 1969, which consisted of 25 members, and General Mahamed Siyaad Barre who was to be its chairman. The next task was to appoint a 15-man Council of Secretaries to run the day-to-day workings of the state. These were young civil servants selected for their ability rather than the traditional clan balancing.

The civilian district and regional governors were replaced by young army and police officers.

The SRC received wide popular support as it embarked on revitalizing the country's economy. It introduced the First Charter of The Revolution, which emphasised the principle of social justice, the stimulation of economic growth, the eradication of tribalism and the setting up of an orthography for the Somali language.

A new chapter was unfolding for the Somalis. Their recently born democracy was being uprooted. They could not know where the "bloodless coup" was to usher them.

---

9. Ibid, p.20.

Chapter V

THE MILITARY GOVERNMENT (1969-1991)

The military junta spoke of a national unity that transcended clannism. For the first time in the short history of the republic, a government was formed without clan affiliation, through which many ministerial portfolios went to civilians. It officially banned clannism in 1971 when effigies representing tribalism were symbolically burned and buried. The word *jaalle* (comrade) was to replace the term *ina adeer* (cousin) and *adeer* (uncle) which was the traditional way to address people.

Adopting a national orthography had been a thorny issue since the inception of the Somali Republic.[10] Even though the

---

10. See *The Peoples of the Horn of Africa: Somali, Afar and Saho*, new eds. (London: Haan Associates for the International African

Osmania script had gained currency in some circles since the early forties, and the Somali Youth League had made it, pre-independence, its official orthography, the civilian government was never able to approve it as the national orthography. The reasons were several: (i) accepting Osmania was seen by some politicians as accepting a clan dominance, as the script was associated with the tribe of its author, Osman Yusuf Kenadid, who was a Majeerteen; (ii) religious sentiments and the pressure for Arabisation was very strong, and led some politicians to favour the Arabic orthography over the indigenous one; and (iii) some educationalists argued that Osmania would be expensive to develop, and they advocated use of the Latin characters.

In 1972 the military regime succeeded in adopting a new orthography where others had failed. It used Latin characters. And on 8 March 1973, a literary campaign was launched with a much publicized motto *"Hadaad taqaan bar"* (if you are literate teach); *"Hadaadan aqoon baro"* (if you are illiterate learn).

The self-help scheme (*iskaa wax-u-qabso*), which was one of the most important features of the Government's political programme, was intended to develop a social and economic infrastructure. It proved very useful in the first few years as it concentrated on the construction of schools, roads and clinics.

The regime ruled by decree approved by the SRC, and controlled the executive, legislative and judicial organs. It introduced sweeping legal and administrative reforms, and carried out extensive social, political and economical

---

Institute), 1994, p.12.

programmes. Underlying the regime's extensive reforms was the control of the people in the name of national security, and the consolidation of the power of the SRC, and in particular of its chairman, General Siyaad Barre. A dictatorial form of authority was in the making. The people could not perceive this. The SRC initiatives created the impression that the military government was more decisive than the civilian rulers had been. Party politics had disappointed and divided society, the ineptitude of the civilian government had left the people disillusioned. Now there was a feeling that the army, which was apart from politics, had rescued the country and prevented it from plunging into turmoil.

The Rhetoric of Scientific Socialism

On the first anniversary of the revolution, 21 October 1970, the SRC Chairman, General Siyaad Barre declared "Scientific Socialism" (*Hantiwadaagga Cilmiga-ku-dhisan*) to be the ideology of the regime and the basis of its social, economical and political programme. Nonetheless, the idea of sharing public property scared the people and to calm them the regime put an acceptable spin on Scientific Socialism, describing it as "simply a modern version of Somali tradition and custom of sharing."

The declared SRC concept of a "modern socialist country" included the eradication of tribalism in favour of nationalism. Effigies of monsters symbolising tribalism were buried at huge rallies held in all regional capitals of the country in 1971. The traditional affiliation of the individual to his clan or lineage, which established a person's social identity and clan alliance, was banned.

The early liberal ideology of the modern Somali state, which later degenerated into tribal polity, had now been replaced by a socialist ideology. The Leftist intellectuals of the previous Somali Democratic Union (SDU) and Hawl iyo Hantiwadaag parties found their opportunity in the new political climate.

Included amongst them were Abdiasis Nuur Hersi, leader of the Hawl iyo Hantiwadaag, Warsame Ali "Juguf", Dr Mahamed Adan Sheikh, Mahamed Yusuf Weyrah, Abdiraxman Aydiid and others. The Leftist intelligentsia became the machine behind government policy in the early years. They were behind the extremist communist policies of the regime in its early stages, such as the solidarity with international socialist countries. But they soon fell out with the regime. Some were accused of going faster than *kacaanka* (the revolution).[11] Others were accused of straying from the revolutionary "tune".[12]

A Public Relation Office (PRO) was formed in 1974, to indoctrinate the masses with the new ideology. It would do this through a network of Orientation Centres (Golaha Hanuuninta) which were set up throughout the country. In government work places "orientation" classes were routine as promotion of government employees depended more on political correctness than competence. Government employees, traders, students, ordinary members of the public, as well as members of women's organizations were forced to attend their neighbourhood orientation centres. For the indoctrination

---

11. Somali version: "Kacaankay ka dheereeyeen."
12. Somali version of "Kacaankay ka gaabiyeen."

of civil servants there was Halane, a military camp south of Muqdisho.

The development of the new ideology was reinforced by depicting General Siyaad Barre as a national cult figure, a ploy used in many communist countries. General Siyaad was symbolised as the saviour of the Somali nation. Names like Victorious Leader (Guulwade) and the Father of the Nation were attributed to the General. A former minister in his government said that the General had three things in common with the Prophet Mahamed: his name, Mahamed, his wife Khadija, and the timing of his leadership when the Somali nation was in danger.

Top priority was given to the establishment of a strong intelligence network. The National Security Service (NSS) dealt with whomever was suspected of nurturing anti-revolutionary feeling. Throughout the 1970s until the mid-1980s, the head of NSS was General Ahmed Saleebaan Abdalla, known as Dafle. He was a son-in-law of the General and also a member of SRC. Because of the NSS's arbitrary powers to arrest, a person could be arrested following a denunciation by his personal enemies. To legitimise its action, all individuals' rights were suspended.[13] The NSS had a network of informers in all public offices, schools and work places.

The first decree of the regime, Law No.1 of 10 January 1970, gave the NSS, as well as Regional and District Revolutionary Councils the power to detain those found (1) to be dangerous to peace, order and good government, and

---

13. Cabdulqaadir Shire Faarax, *Xeebtii Geerida*, London, July 90, pp.118-120.

(2) to be conspiring against the SRC by word or by action.[14] In the following years more repressive laws and institutions were created. Among these were the *Hangash* which was Military Intelligence, *Dhabar Jebin*, the Military Counter-Intelligence, and *Baarista Xisbiga*, the Party Investigators.

By this time conflict had occurred between the civilian administrators and the military officers. The civilian intellectuals, who were the educated élite of the society, expected to be the policy-makers of the Government. This was at odds with the military who regarded themselves as the force behind change. In fact the military officers saw the civilian administrators simply as their subordinates. The two groups clashed and naturally the intellectuals lost the battle, many of them ending up in prison. Others, such as Dr Hassan Ali Mire (Minister of Education), Avv. Mahamud Ghelle (Minister of Information) and Abdalla Farah Hersi (Minister of Agriculture), resigned from the cabinet.

From this point General Siyaad Barre became more sensitive to criticism and slowly he dropped from office all leftist intellectuals - who until now had been the ideological backbone of his rule. Some were arrested and others fled to South Yemen, where they formed the Somali Workers Party (SWP) and the Somali Democratic Liberation Front (SDLF). Barre replaced them with politicians ready to serve him.

To reinforce the National Security Service, a National Security Court (NSC) was created in 1970. The NSC was headed by General Mahamud Ghelle Yusuf who had never read law. No appeal could be made against the verdict of the

---

14. An African Watch Report, Somalia: A Government at War with its Own People, January 1990, p.16.

NSC. The court dealt with all political cases, and matters pertaining to public order and murder.

The Victorious Pioneers (*Guulwadayaal*), a large paramilitary force established in 1972 and drawn from the nation's youth, acted as the regime's watchdog at neighbourhood level. The head of the Victories Pioneers was Abdurahman 'Guulwade', son-in-law of the President. Its powers of arrest were independent of the regular police force.

The regime also took drastic measures to curb the development of independent intellectual thought or artistic talent.[15] However, in response to this oppression the leading Somali poets, Mahamed Warsame "Hadraawi" and Mahamed Haashi Dhamac "Gaariye" challenged the regime with their poetic talent when they began the famous poetic chain called "Deelley". Deelley expressed the people's feelings toward the regime's policy.

The jubilant welcome, which the *coup d'etat* initially received, gradually declined and changed to fear. Family members and neighbours were encouraged to spy on each other and report to the Victory Pioneers. The song *Your shadow is watching you*[16] was meant to intimidate people from drifting from the revolutionary path.

The nepotism of the regime retribalied Somali politics to an extent never before seen, and created maximum suspicion and mistrust among Somali clans. No group could trust

---

15. Ibid., p.26. See also Maxamed D. Afrax, Culture and Catastrophe in Somalia: the Search for a New Discourse, A paper presented at *The Somali Challenge: Peace, Resources and Reconstruction*, Geneva on 10-14 July 1992.

16. The Somali version of the revolutionary song *"Harkaagaa laguu diray"*.

another. People were persecuted for their political ideals, and some disappeared.[17]

Despite emphasising the creation of an egalitarian society, the military government controlled every aspect of an individual's life. The political pattern of the regime - curbing the right of assembly, making attendance at orientation centres compulsory, the arbitrary powers of arrest, conflicted with the egalitarianism of traditional Somali culture.[18] As a result of this policy thousands of educated men and women fled the country resulting in a brain drain.

Barre's Grip on Power

The enormous powers conferred on the chairman of the SRC enabled General Barre to stifle any immediate threat to his authority. On 20 April 1970 he arrested the first Vice-President, General Jama Ali Khorshel accusing him of an attempted coup. General Khorshel was fortunate to escape the firing squad. However, a year later General Salaad Gabayre Kediye, Minister of Defence and a senior SRC member, General Mahamed Aynanshe, the Vice-President, also an SRC senior member, and Colonel Abdulqadir Dheel, a former army officer, were accused of trying to depose General Barre. They were arrested in 1971 and executed by a firing squad on 23 July, 1972 in Muqdisho.

There are conflicting opinions as to the reason behind the executions of the three men. General Barre became distrustful

---

17. Rashid Maxamed "Gambon", The Anatomy of The Civil War: Somalia in Post-Independence" in *Conference on Current Events in Somalia*, Nairobi, 18 October 1993.
18. I M Lewis, *A Modern History of Somalia*, op. cit., p. 211.

of the young officers, especially General Salaad Gabayre Kediye who was believed to be one of the architects of the October *coup d'etat*. Another opinion was that the execution was a message to the clans to which the three belonged. General Gabayre hailed from the Abgaal clan, which forms the majority of the Hawiye clans; General Aynanshe belonged to the Habar Yonis (Isaaq) and Colonel Abdulqadir Dheel was from the Majeerteen (Daarood) — the first victims of General Barre's repressive campaign. Whatever the reason, by eliminating these men, General Barre was to become the indisputable leader of the SRC.

The MOD Constellation

By eliminating any threat to his power, from July 1972 Barre covertly embarked upon building his power base on an alliance with two other clan groups. This was what was to become known as the MOD.[19] The MOD alliance, which the General formulated to rule the country is the acronym for the Mareehaan (Barre's paternal relatives), the Ogaadeen (his mother's relatives) and Dhulbahante (his son-in-law's clan). However, he met resistance from intellectuals and traditional leaders among the MOD, some of whom had suffered and had been imprisoned. For instance, Abdi Hashi Dhorre, of the Mareehaan, was confined to prison in Iskushuban in the Bari region for his opposition to the General's policy. Another well-known leader was the nationalist Garaad of the Dhulbahante, Ali Garaad Jama, who died whilst in exile in Egypt in the early 1980s. Garaad Ali (also known as

---

19. Said Samatar and David Laitan, *Somalia: Nation in Search of a State, op. cit.*, p.94.

Garaad of the Harti) was one of the few traditional Somali clan leaders with college education.

The MOD alliance became a political instrument whose effect was to build up resentment among other clan groupings.

By firmly establishing his inner power structure, Barre started to deploy a two-tier system, one which rewarded some sub-clans for their loyalty to the *Kacaanka Barakaysan* (the Blessed Revolution), and the other to persecute and repress those sub-clans "for their recalcitrance or reluctance to be enthusiastic about the new order imposed upon them."[20] The first group who fell under the guillotine of this campaign was the Majeerteen clan.

The government policy to alienate a section of the society (as collective punishment) was responsible for the decline of the government ability to enforce law and stability, and to mobilize support for its policy. When a group is threatened with coercion, the threat may bring the group together and they may respond with counter-coercion. This reaction may then produce an intensifying of this initial coercion. The result may be an endless upward spiral of aggressive tactics.[21] In fact, these tactics generated and increased people's awareness of clan identity.

Superpower Rivalry in the Horn

At the turn of the century the main colonialists in the Horn were Britain, Germany, France and Italy. As colonies became independent, the mode of competition changed to

---

20. Siciid Faarax Maxamuud, Prisoners of Siyadist Culture in *Hal-Abuur*, Vol I, No. 1, Summer 1993, p.17.
21. Dolf Zillmann, Hostility and Aggression, *op. cit.* pp.120-200.

influencing countries indirectly rather than the establishment of direct control as was the case in the colonial era.

During the Cold War, the Horn of Africa's strategic location near the oil-rich Middle East was of great value to the superpowers. To further their strategic interest, both the former Soviet Union and the United States took advantage of the vulnerability of the Somali-Ethiopian dispute, heightening the volatile relationship of the Horn of Africa states in the 1970s and early 1980s. The resulting rivalry created a situation whereby the superpowers poured substantial economic and military assistance into this region. This in turn fomented the Ethiopian and Somali territorial dispute.

Both the Ethiopian and Somali internal political perspectives have been heavily distorted by the colonial legacy. To further their interests in the region, the superpowers favoured strong leadership. It is believed that the Soviet Union was involved in the military takeover in October 1969 in Somalia, and later, in 1974 in Ethiopia. Suspicion over this claim spread when the Soviet Union was the first country to welcome both coups.

Since the last century, this part of the world has rarely witnessed peace, until new boundaries appeared — witnessing the birth of the Eritrean Republic in 1992. Looking from this perspective, peace and stability are still a long way away in this region, and this has repercussions for international peace.

The Impact of the Cold War on the Horn

The Soviet naval base at Berbera, which was built in the early 1970s, was considered by the United States and its allies as a threat to vital western security interests in the Gulf and

Indian Ocean regions. The Soviets had a communication centre at Kismaayo, in the southern part of the country near the border with Kenya. They built at Berbera, on the Red Sea, a dry dock, missile handling and storage facilities, a communication station, large fuel facilities, and a 15,000-foot runway capable of accommodating large Soviet aircraft.[22] In Armis, near Muqdisho, they also built a giant radar and other communication receiver facilities and transmitter sites.

To counter the Soviet presence in the Horn, the United States administration was pressing the American Congress to fund the expansion of naval facilities on the Indian Ocean island of Diego Garcia (leased by Britain in 1965).

The United States established a military presence in the Horn in the 1950s, when it built a military communication base at Kagnew in Eritrea (then a province of Ethiopia, Eritrea now an independent state). With the acquisition of the facilities at Diego Garcia, which was nearer to the Gulf region, the United States lost interest in Kagnew.

To woo Somalia into switching from the Soviet sphere, in 1975 Saudi Arabia offered to take over economic aid projects then financed by Moscow, and to buy US arms for Somalia in order to replace the Soviet weapons.[23] In obscure circumstances, however, the then US Secretary of State, Henry Kissinger, objected to the Saudi Arabian idea. The possible reason for Kissinger's opposition to Somalia switching to the western camp was that if the Soviets were expelled from Somalia at that time, it would be difficult for

---

22. Samuel M Makinda, *Seeking Peace From Chaos*, 1993, pp.52-3.
23. Ibid., pp.52-54.

the United States administration to convince Congress to approve funds for the expansion of Diego Garcia facilities.

Exploring the possibility of influencing Somali leaders, in 1977, the US government started sending signals to Somalia to supply arms during the Somali-Ethiopian war of 1977-1978 (also know as the Ogaadeen War). However, the US government was cautious of not igniting sensitive issues such as that of boundaries or territorial issues. Basically the boundary issues were considered as a serious threat to the existence of many states in Africa. Many African states were vulnerable and suspicious of any challenge to the colonially defined boundaries, fearing that the framework of existing political equation in the continent might be swept away in an anarchy of nationalism and other conflicts.[24] Despite knowing Ethiopia's colonial past, African politicians preferred to ignore Ethiopia's past roles. Somalia, in the eyes of many African countries, was considered to be the aggressor trying to impose its territorial boundary on Ethiopia by force. Against this political background, in August 1977 the United States decided not to give Somalia arms.

Following the Iranian revolution and the Soviet intervention in Afghanistan, the Carter administration signed agreements with Somalia, Kenya and Sudan to gain access to their military facilities.[25] The agreement allowed the United States to use the former Soviet base at Berbera for what was to become the newly formed Rapid Development Task Force in 1980.

Table 1 - **The Economy: Major Characteristics of Official**

---

24. Alfred Gobban, *National Self-determination,,* 1945, P.31.
25. Ibid., p.55.

Accounts and Actual Behaviour in 1977-1983.

Characteristics	Official Accounts	Actual Behaviour
1977-1983		
1. Migration reaches 1500.000 + workers "franco valuta" system Remittances US$400 million.	1. Per capita income stagnant	1. Per capital income rose
2. Major drought income	2. Livestock exports stagnant after 1977	2. Pastoralist from exports rose dramatically
3. War in Ogaadeen	3. Remittence $40 million per year	3. Current account of balance of payment positive.
4. Rupture with the collapsing, boom in became	4. Deterioration in sector USSR. informal trading	4. Urban formal current account activities major source of family income (remittance effect).
5. Export boom for livestock sector	5. Formal sector wage declines dramatically	
6. Stagnation in urban formal sector		

Source: Inter-Disciplinary Employment and Project, ILO/JASPA, 1989, p.5.

Declining Food Production

Within the framework of capitalism and colonialism, the economic map of the world was redrawn. Many countries were forced into producing for the sake of competing in international trade. In Somalia the banana was grown for such purposes. The same thing happened, not only in other African countries, but also in Latin America, Asia and the Pacific Islands. Many scholars pointed out that the colonialists' emphasis on cash crops and competitive produce helped to dismantle the traditional way of farming, thereby weakening the land, the food chain and the means of coping with drought.

In Somalia, for example, at the end of the 1930s, a sizeable Italian population settled as farmers in the area between the two rivers, Jubba and Shabeelle. However, the settlers needed a work force for their huge plantations. For the local inhabitants, waged work was alien. To recruit a work force, the Italian colonial authority passed a law compelling the local inhabitants to work on the farms. In 1938 an even more rigid system was introduced by the fascist Government. Control of trade and commerce were taken over by government monopolies and para-statal organizations. The system excluded Somali or colonial "subjects" in any sector of the economy where they might be in competition with Italians.[26]

In 1970 and 1972, in order to secure public ownership of the means of production in the light of Scientific Socialism, the military regime nationalised banking and insurance institutions and industry. Finally in 1974 the shipping lines were also stateowned. The National Agency for Commerce (ENC) was established to monopolise wholesale trade. The regime introduced forced collectivisation of Somali peasants (the Crash Programme). At the same time, the military government forced local farmers to sell their grain products to

---

26. I M Lewis, *A Modern History of Somalia, op. cit.*, p.110-12.

a state enterprise, the Agricultural Development Corporation (ADC). The ADC's price for grain was lower than the free market price, forcing the farmers to change their production to cash crops such as tomatoes, cabbage, watermelon, etc. It has been asserted by several donor agencies, the World Bank particularly, that the monopoly role of the ADC discouraged grain production and created "distortions" that misallocated resources.[27]

Declining local food production, meant that in mid-1970s Somalia began to import more food than in the previous decade. From this time Somalia became more vulnerable to famine.

At the end of the 1980s Somalia was suffering a severe case of economic imbalance. This condition forced the state into fiscal bankruptcy and the Gross National Product was destroyed. Consequently, while the state of the economy was lowering the standard of living, hyperinflation was wiping out the value of the national currency.

From this time Barre's two-tier policy — rewarding exorbitantly some groups for their loyalty to him and victimising those whom he suspected of being against his regime — was in shambles, as his regime was susceptible to any alteration to the external assistance which was its lifeline.

---

27. *Generating Employment and Income in Somalia*, Report of an ILO/JASPA Inter-Disciplinary Employment and Project-Identification Mission to Somalia, ILO, United Nations Development Programme, Addis Ababa, 1989, p.9.

Chapter VI
THE IMPACT OF THE WAR

From its inception, the military government undertook a vast international campaign to denounce the colonial behaviour of Ethiopia towards the Somalis in Western Somaliland. Under the auspices of the OAU, a new dialogue was opened between Somalia and Ethiopia in 1971, but at the end of 1972 the two parties' positions were so far apart that negotiations failed. Ethiopia reinforced its military presence along the border with Somalia. Kenya did the same. Feeling the threat, Somalia took the matter to the OAU.

Instability in the Ethiopian Political Establishment

In 1974 a new political horizon was looming for Ethiopia as Emperor Haile Selassie's feudal monarchy was crippled by waves of demonstrations organized by the Ethiopian People's

Revolutionary Party (EPRP), the Ethiopian Democratic Union (EDU), students, teachers and workers' groups. Haile Selassie sent his troops to quell the demonstrations. However, this caused more resentment. Soon the situation got out of hand. On 12 September, 1974 the Ethiopian army took advantage of the deteriorating circumstances and deposed the Emperor, who had ruled Ethiopia for four decades.

The change of government heralded a change in political ideology. The Soviet Union who was monitoring the situation, found a breeding ground for its ideology with the military regime which showed communist tendencies. In view of the new political atmosphere in the region, the Soviet strategists sensed a new opportunity: to expand Soviet influences by creating a "Pax-Sovietica" federation based on Marxist-Leninist ideology among Somalia, Ethiopia and the People's Democratic Republic of Yemen. In March 1976 Fidel Castro began to realize this plan by paying official visits to the region. However, the plan failed when Somalia insisted that the Western Somaliland issue be solved before any confederation was created.

Meanwhile, in Ethiopia the political situation was worsening as General Aman Andom, the chairman of the Dergue (the Ethiopian Revolutionary Government) was killed, along with some 60 high ranking officials, and replaced by General Tafari Banti. After a short time, a group led by Lieutenant Colonel Mengistu Haile Mariam eliminated General Tafari Banti and took power.

The Ethiopian-Somali War

The political turmoil in Ethiopia gave Somalia a chance to retake the missing territory. In July 1977, the Somali government decided to commit its army to the liberation of Western Somaliland and to help the Western Somali Liberation Front (WSLF) which had increased its operations since the beginning of the 1970s. Backed by the Somali army, WSLF launched a massive offensive and liberated nearly all the Somali-inhabited Western Somaliland within a short time by capturing main towns such as Jigjiga, Goday (Gode), Dhagahbuur, and, very briefly, Dire Dawa.

Menaced internally as well as externally, the military regime in Addis Ababa declared itself a Marxist-Leninist state, and appealed to the Soviet Union for military assistance. As a result, the Soviet Union shifted its alliance from Somalia to Ethiopia by moving its military advisers from Muqdisho and directly flew them to Addis Ababa in a back-stabbing policy, which Lewis described as "one of the most breathtaking acts of treachery in history."[1]

In reaction to the Soviet Union tactics, on 13 November, 1977 Somalia abrogated the 10-year Treaty of Friendship and Cooperation signed in 1974, and ordered all Soviets to leave the country within 17 days. General Barre turned to the West and to the moderate Arab countries for military and financial help.

The Soviet Union had reinforced the Ethiopian army with 18,000 Cuban soldiers, along with Yemeni and East German technicians, allowing it to severely defeat the Somali army

---

1. I M Lewis, In the Land of the Living Dead, *The Sunday Times*, 30 August 1992.

and in March 1978 Somalia ordered its remaining army in the war to retreat.

The defeat had tremendous impact on the Somali psyche and morale which was to linger with them for the rest of their lives, as the great composer and poet Ali Sugulle echoes in his poem:

> So long as the moon is not full
> Nor the star complete
> So long as fate lingers on her travels
> I will neither exalt my culture
> Nor seek worldly goods[0]

The Aftermath of the Ethiopian-Somali War

Economically, socially, politically and ecologically the war had profound consequences (Table 2). Development project funds were diverted to the war. The wave of refugees, estimated to be more than a million, required financial assistance which the country could not afford at all. To cope with the new situation, Somalia had to rely on foreign aid. It was the beginning of the pauperization policy of Somalia.

Many refugees from the contested Western Somaliland and adjacent areas now flowed into the Republic. These surges of refugees were accompanied by a flood of modern weapons from the war front in Ethiopia into the country: a wave that was to transform Somalia.[2]

On the other hand, thousands of pastoral Somalis fled from Western Somaliland with their animal stock into Somalia, creating over-grazing in many areas. The result was disastrous

---

2. Quoted in "The Ogaden Conflict 1977-1978" documentary video.

ecologically and produced conditions never experienced before in the country.

The Ethiopian-Somali War, also known as the Ogaadeen War,[3] abruptly heightened the stature of the General within the country. However, the defeat generated dissatisfaction and despondency within the army. The backlash troubled General Siyaad Barre. To counter any attempt to show resistance within the army, a few days before the retreat from Ethiopia, six high ranking army officers accused of disobedience were executed in Hargeysa military camp after a secret trial. As further intimidation, General Mahamed Ali Samatar and his Joint North Army Commander,[4] General Mahamud Nuur Galaal, executed 82 commissioned and non-commissioned officers in Jigjiga for what the regime justified as "their opposition to the way the war was handled." In reality, the shot officers were said to be among the best men of the troops. The policy was a wide tactic to quell any attempt at opposition from the army.

General Siyaad's much feared nightmare appeared to have come true when on 9 April, 1978 a coup, led by Colonel Mahamed Sheikh Osman "Irro", was attempted and rebel troops took control of the capital. Nevertheless, the coup proved to be ill-planned and abortive; by mid-morning troops loyal to General Siyaad Barre had contained the situation and rounded up some of the ring-leaders in an operation which

---

3. I M Lewis, In the Land of the Living Dead, *The Sunday Times,* 30 August 1992.

4. Due to military requirement at the time of the Ogaadeen War the Somali military forces were divided into two fronts: the Joint Northern Army led by General Maxamuud Galaal and the Joint Southern Army led by Colonel Cabdullaahi Yuusuf Axmed.

led to the death of 28 people. However, the mastermind of the coup, Colonel Abdullahi Yusuf Ahmed, the South Front Commander, fled to Nairobi with six other associates. And on 13 September 1978 Colonel Mahamed Sheikh Osman "Irro" and sixteen other officers were condemned to death by the National Security court and they were executed on 26 October 1978 — 34 people were imprisoned from 10 to 20-year term.[5]

The Formation of the Armed Opposition

If the Ogaadeen War enhanced the prestige of the General within the country, its loss triggered the attempted coup on 9 April 1978, which the General cunningly portrayed as a clan's attempt to take over power. On the one hand, the failed coup attempt was exploited by the General to divert the country's misery from his failed policies and by using as a scapegoat the ring leader's kin (the Majeerteen). On the other hand, in order to avoid any future attempt on his regime, it provided Barre with a chance to reconstruct the military using his inner kinsmen, and thereby, estranging other groups.

In response to the coup, harsh reprisals were carried out upon the accused men's kin, the Majeerteen. Because of this retribution, the first armed opposition movement, the Somali Salvation Front (SSF) was formed on 8 February, 1979,[6] by Colonel Abdullahi Yusuf Ahmed, Osman Nuur Ali Qonof, a former Supreme Court Judge (1969-70), who had also

---

5. Amnesty International Report, AI Index: Afr 52/11/85, July 1985.
6. An Africa Watch Report, *Somalia: A Government at War with its Own People, 1990, op. cit.*, p.29.

been General-Secretary of the defunct Somali Democratic Action Front (SODAF) (an opposition movement formed in Addis Ababa in 1976) Mustafa Haji Nuur, a well-known broadcaster, and Omar Hassan Mahamed (Omar Stalin), a former Mayor of Muqdisho. The era of challenges to the rule of General Barre had begun. When people are persecuted and not given a chance to express their grievances, it is natural to look for a mechanism to show their feelings. The armed resistance groups, which started to form at the end of the 1970s in neighbouring Ethiopia, became the means to express this and it was also a trend that was to transform Somalia.

"The Accursed Days" in the North-Eastern Regions

With the help of Ethiopia, the SSF started their raids inside the country by attacking government installations. To deprive the SSF of political and social support,[7] the regime used a scorched-earth policy in the Mudug, Nugaal and Bari regions[8] and parts of Jubba region. Whenever the SSF launched its operations inside the country, the regime retaliated against what the regime called "SSF kinsmen". The regime rounded up hundreds of Majeerteen officers and unfolded its propaganda machine to justify their persecution. The persecution took place on every level. It purged the civil service. Prominent politicians, traditional leaders, intellectuals

---

7. SSF (later SSDF) draws its support from the Majeerteen and their relative Arab Salah (Meheri) who majority live in Mudug, Nugal and Bari regions, (known also North-Eastern region during the civil war)) and in Kismayo in the south.
8. An Africa Watch Report, *Somalia: A Government at War with its Own People, 1990*, op. cit., p.29.

and businessmen and women of the Majeerteen were sent to the infamous dreadful Labaatan Jirow prison in the Bay region and Laanta Buur near Marka. Some of them died in detention. Colonel Jama Ali Jama and Lawyer Bar-da'ad, who became the longest serving political prisoners in Somalia, were recognised by Amnesty International as prisoners of conscience.[9] As the Government became alarmed by the threat of an armed insurgency, it tightened control of the Majeerteen country. Emergency regulations were put into effect in the Mudug, Nugaal and Bari in the north-east regions and Kismaayo area. The security forces and the military were given extensive powers under the emergency regulations.[10] In 1981, 25 students were arrested in Garowe, capital of the Nugaal Region, after they were accused of distributing seditious pamphlets. Ten of the students were sentenced to death; the others were given life imprisonment and long sentences. To bring the centuries old trade of the Bari region with the Arabian Peninsula to its knees, the regime seized at least 20 commercial boats and banned all kinds of trade in these parts thus causing massive exodus from the Majeerteen country leaving some urban areas as ghost towns. Schools and hospitals in Galkayo, Garowe, Qardho, Iskushuban, Bosaso, Alula, Khandala, Bandar Beyla, Burtinle and Jarriban districts were closed and some of them razed to deprive the people of these basic services.

To squeeze the Somali regime, in June 1982 SSF launched an offensive capturing Balan-balle and Geel-dogob, towns in

---

9. Amnesty International Report, AI Index: Afr 52/11/85, July 1985.
10. I M Lewis, *A Modern History of Somalia*, rev. ed. *op. cit.*, pp.252-53.

the central regions. Again in reprisal the army made massive onslaughts in the Mudug, Nugaal and Bari regions, destroying water reservoirs,[11] burning 18 villages, among them Ba'aadweyn, Balli-busle, Tuula Jalam, Xaraf, Bayra, Gambarrey and Riigoomane. They also planted land mines around main towns and confiscated thousands of livestock.

The anguish which the people of this region felt was voiced by Khalif Sheikh Mahamud in his poem Hurgomo:[12]

> It may be the Lord's ordained will that
> The Majeerteen should be consumed like honey
> Like the wild berries in the plain of Do'aan,
> The Majeerteen have been greedily devoured,
> Every hungry man in the land desired to bite off
> A piece of flesh from the prostrated body of the
> Majeerteen.

Both the urban population and nomads were subject to summary arrest, detention in squalid conditions, torture, rape, and all forms of psychological intimidation. In what Said Samatar calls *maalmo inkaaran* (the accursed days) of May-June 1979, the Red Berets (*Koofiyad Guduud or Koofiyad Cas*) created carnage in the Mudug and Nugaal regions where more than 2000 Majeerteen died as a result of thirst

---

11. Reservoirs (berkedo) are dug out of the ground to collect water during the rainy season. The water is used by people and animals during the dry season (Jiilaal).

12. Said S Samatar, *Somalia: A Nation in Turmoil*, The Minority Rights Group, London, 1991, p.19. The Somali version of the poem:
   Majeerteen Ilaah wuxuu ka dhigay malab sidiisiiye
   Sida miraha Doocaan ka baxa muudsay aadmiguye
   Nin waliba wuxuu mihindisaa inuu magowshaaye.

and sun exposure[13] after their water reservoir *(berkedo)* were destroyed.[14] In the same operation, the Red Berets engaged in massive looting by seizing 50,000 camels, 10,000 head of cattle and 100,000 sheep and goats.[15] Meanwhile, in October 1981 the SSF fused with two leftist movements, the Somali Workers Party (SWP) led by Said Jama Husein, and the Somali Democratic Liberation Front (SDLF), led by Abdiraxman Aydiid, to form a larger national opposition movement, and changed its name to Somali Salvation Democratic Front (SSDF).

The pattern of abuse directed at the Majeerteen clan was a calamitous omen of what was in store for the Somali clans, especially for the Isaaq people[16], whose plight caused the foundation (in London) in April, 1981 of the Isaaq-based Somali National Movement (SNM) by prominent Isaaq politicians. Suspecting every Isaaq of supporting the SNM, the regime unleashed a reign of terror on the Isaaq population.

The reign of terror began on 27 February, 1982 with measures against Isaaq intellectuals calling themselves "the Hargeysa Group" who were accused of belonging to an illegal organization called "Men Born in the City" (*Ragga U-Dhashay-Magaalada*).[17] Riots led by students broke out outside the National Security Court, and the Red Berets were

---

13. Said S Samatar, *Somalia: A Nation in Turmoil*, A Minority Rights Group, August 1991, pp.35-45.
14. Ibid. pp.36-45.
15. Ibid. pp.36-45.
16. Ibid., p.29.
17. An African Watch Report, Somalia: A Government at War with its Own People, January 1990, p.37.

called in to quell the protesters. Consequently, the Red Berets fired on the unarmed demonstrators, killing five people.[18]

The trial lasted for two days. Three of the group members were sentenced to life imprisonment, and 18 other defendants where given sentences of between three to thirty years.[19]

Meanwhile, the SNM was carrying out daring guerrilla operations in the north. They released Isaaq political prisoners from Mandhera (Mandera) Central prison in the north on 2 January 1983.

The 1979 Constitution

Anxious to get military and economic assistance from the West after the shift of alliance from the Soviet Union, and to forestall opposition movements, General Siyaad Barre announced a new constitution in 1979. The referendum on the new constitution was held on 29 August, 1979 and, as reported by the Gitution reaffirmed Scientific Socialism as the guiding ideology of the regime and the Somali Revolutionary Socialist Party as the sole political party.

The constitution, which was supposed to "fit the ill intentions of the military revolutionary council",[20] came into effect in the following month, and on 30 December an election was held for the 171 members of the People's Assembly (Golaha Ummadda) as the parliament became known. The election was entirely different from the last

---

18. Ibid., p.39.
19. Ibid., pp.38-9.
20. Rashid Maxamed "Gambon", The Anatomy of The Civil War: Somalia in Post-Independence" in *Conference on Current Events in Somalia*, Nairobi, 18 October 1993.

democratic election under the civilian government, in which candidates competed for seats in Parliament. In this election the SRSP nominated the members and presented them in a single list to the electorate.

Finally, in January 1980 the new assembly held its first session and elected General Siyaad Barre as president of the Republic for a seven year term. For the first time the military rank was removed from his title.

The Somali-Ethiopian Peace Agreement

While General Siyaad Barre was fighting his war, Lieutenant Colonel Mengistu Haile Mariam of Ethiopia was destabilized by the conflicts in Eritrea and in Western Somaliland. In 1984 Mengistu failed in a much publicised campaign called the Red Star, which was to wipe out the Eritrean Liberation Front (ELF) and the Eritrean People's Liberation Front (EPLP) which had taken control of Karen, an important and strategic position in Eritrea. He wanted desperately to transfer the Eastern Army, which guarded the front with Somalia, to Eritrea.

Using the two Somali towns of Balan Balle and Geeldogob which had been controlled by the SSDF, with the help of the Ethiopian army since June 1982, as a bargaining counter, in October 1985, Goshe Walde, the Ethiopian Foreign Minister, officially declared these two towns part of Ethiopia. And in reaction, Colonel Abdullahi Yusuf Ahmed, the SSDF chairman, countered furiously against the minister's assertion by announcing the two towns as part and parcel of Somalia's territory. Following this controversy, the Ethiopian authorities ordered his arrest and subsequently they killed five of his bodyguards in Dire Dawa.

Both tottering in the face of internal dissent, General Siyaad Barre and Lieutenant Colonel Mengistu Haile Mariam needed hostilities between the two countries to cease and the policy of helping each other's dissident groups to be stopped. Aiming to ease their respective anxiety, they first met in Djibouti at the Inter-Governmental Authority for Drought and Development (IGADD) in January 1986 under the auspices of President Hassan Guled Abtidon of Djibouti, but without concluding an agreement. The difference over how to tackle border issue derailed it. Again they met on 6 April, 1988, and this time they signed an agreement that included the end by both parties of any support for the opposition of the other.[21]

To get the quickest benefit from their agreement, Haile Mariam immediately ordered the closure of SSDF and SNM radio, Radio Halgan.[22] Then he rounded up the remaining SSDF leaders and their heavy weapons, some of which had been obtained from Libya.

Taking advantage of the SSDF fate, the SNM was more vigilant and decided to move its forces inside the country in a vast offensive on the Somali regime installations in May 1988. On 27 May they seized Bur-o' (Bura-o) and after four

---

21. Mahamed Osman Omar, *The Road to Zero, op. cit*, pp.186-188.
22. Previously the radio was know as Radio Kulmis when it was used only by the SSDF when it started its struggle from Ethiopia in February 1979. As the SNM started its struggle again Barre's regime in 1981, the radio had to be jointly used by the two movements, thus giving the name Radio Halgan.

days they took control of half of Hargeysa. The powerful Sector 26 June Army crumbled in front of the SNM forces.

To crush the resistance, the regime sent its troops to the north ordering them to retake the towns using all means. However, unable to defeat the SNM in direct combat, the troops turned their firepower, including their air force and artillery, against the Isaaq civilians, causing an unimaginable death toll. Some have estimated more than 10,000 dead and 30,000 wounded. And more than 350,000 refugees crossed the border with Ethiopia[23] and Djibouti. After weeks of fighting, with indiscriminate air bombardment, Bur-o' and Hargeysa were reduced to rubble. Civilians fled to the neighbouring countries and on their way they were bombarded by the air force, as a seventy-year old survivor described:

> I never thought that one day it could happen to me that I would flee from the very army created to protect me from enemies, and that it would unleash the scourge of all its firepower on me. I fled from Hargeysa with what remained of my family to the border with Ethiopia. Only at night time we could walk, because during the daytime aeroplane were flying over us and often I could see them bombing human targets.[24]

In an emotional reaction, SNM contingents shot not only government officials, but also many non-Isaaq unarmed civilians, mainly believed to belong Daarood and Gadabuursi

---

23. Ahmed I Samatar, The Curse of Allah: Civic Disembowelment and the Collapse of the State in Somalia, A Paper presented at the Conference on *The Somali Challenge: Peace, Resources, and Reconstruction*, Geneva, Switzerland, 10-14 July 1992, p.42.
24. Ismail Kahin Odawa, field note, Interviewed in Cardiff, Wales, 22 October 1992.

clans. They also attacked a number of refugee camps in which women and children where killed.[25]

When the government troops took control of Bur-o' (Bura-o) and Hargeysa what remained of the two towns was only rubble and havoc.

Conflict in the North

Because of the Ogaadeen War in 1978, a huge influx of refugees of ethnic Somalis and Oromos from Ethiopia came into Somalia. Most of the ethnic Somali refugees who belonged to the Absame (Ogaadeen, Bartire, Abasguul, Jidwaaq, Baal-ad, and Weyteen clans) and Gheri clans (both of the Daarood clan-family) went to refugee camps in the northern part of the country. The Western Somali Liberation Front which fought for the liberation of Western Somaliland found manpower from among the refugees, therefore recruited them.

The Somali constitution granted citizenship to any ethnic Somali born in the lost territories. Although the Somalis from the Western Somaliland were identified as refugees, they were treated as Somali citizens.

Traditionally Ogaadeen and Isaaq nomads met in the Hawd (Haud), a vast territory in the Western Somaliland, to find pasture. When the WSLF recruits began their operation on the border between Ethiopia and Somalia there were many complaints from the Isaaq nomads. The Isaaq blamed the WSLF for siding with their kinsmen, the Ogaadeen, who

---

25. An African Watch Report, Somalia: A Government at War with its Own People, January 1990, p.10.

were Isaaq's traditional rivalries.[26] In September 1979, a group of Isaaq elders passed their grievances to the Government.[27] However, the regime's bungling of the matter fuelled rumours that accused General Siyaad Barre's MOD coalition of planning a policy to settle the Ogaadeen people in the land of Isaaq. The Ogaadeen clan, who form one of the largest Daarood clans the majority of whom live in Western Somaliland, was regarded as one of the pillars of the regime.[28] Isaaq officers, angered by the regime's distrustful policies, began to desert the army to join the SNM, which was established in reaction to the Isaaq grievances. While combatting the regime, the SNM also fought the WSLF.

These circumstances also disrupted Western Somaliland trade with the northern regions, and in November 1982 clan war erupted between the two groups after the Isaaq clans killed Ogaadeen students returning to Western Somaliland.[29] In the following fighting, SNM sided with their kinsmen while WSLF fought for the Ogaadeen clan.

The Débâcle of the MOD Constellation

In June 1986 General Siyaad Barre escaped a near fatal car accident on the road between Muqdisho and Afgooye,

---

26. John Makakis, The Isaq-Ogaden Dispute, in *Ecology and Politics: Environment Stress and Security in Africa*, ed. Anders Hjort af Ornäs et al. *op. cit.*, p.164.
27. An African Watch Report, Somalia: A Government at War with its Own People, January 1990, p.31.
28. John Makakis, The Isaq-Ogaden Dispute, *in Ecology and Politics: Environment Stress and Security in Africa*, ed. Anders Hjort af Ornäs et al., *op. cit.* p.164.
29. Ibid., p.165.

a town 30 kilometres south of Muqdisho. Following the accident, he went into a coma, and was subsequently flown to Riyadh in the personal jet of King Fahad Ibn Abdulasis of Saudi Arabia.[30] To deter any thoughts of a miltary coup, a frantic show of strength was staged by the general's kinsmen, the Mareehaan. This threatening performance sent a clear message to all clans, including the other MOD clans, thus shattering the regime's tribal alliance.

Whatever the reaction, two things became evident. First, the near deadly accident had raised the question of the succession to the General. This political trend excluded the other two MOD coalition members, namely the Ogaadeen and Dhulbahante. Secondly, it showed the breaking up of the coalition which was the backbone of the regime. The traditional Somali clan alliance is always fluid and the MOD was not an exception. The era of the break-up of the MOD's grip on power had begun with the unexpected car accident that sparked the drawn-out demise of the General.

According to Somali constitution, if the head of state loses consciousness, responsibility transfers to the vice-president, who becomes acting president. This should have devolved to the First Vice-President, General Mahamed Ali Samatar. To prevent this from happening, the President's clansmen, who controlled the armed forces, imposed house arrest on General Samatar, along with many members of the Central Committee of the Somali Revolutionary Socialist Party. Samatar tried without success to convene a meeting of the Party.[31]

---

30. Mahamed Osman Omar The Road to Zero, *op. cit*, p.188.
31. Ali Issa-Salwe, field note, interviewed in 3 March 1985, Bombay, India.

The cracks in the coalition had become evident in General Siyaad Barre's peace agreement with Ethiopia. The WSLF regarded the agreement as an abandonment of the Somali people still under colonial rule, and specifically of the inhabitants of Western Somaliland. The Ogaadeen and their kin in the Absame and Geri clans, who make up most of the Western Somaliland inhabitants, gave all their heart to the Western Somaliland struggle. They saw the peace accord as back-stabbing by the regime of which they were one of the pillars.

Another plausible theory has it that the break-up began to develop during the Ogaadeen War. While the Somali army was pushing the Ethiopian out of the Ogaadeen, suspicion emerged about Ogaadeen officers taking advantage of the situation to assume control of the region and form their independent state. It was not a coincidence when the Somali regime nominated a non-Ogaadeen man, Abdirisaq Abubakar, as the Extraordinary Commissioner for the liberated area of the Ogaadeen.[32]

As evidence of the deteriorating relations within the MOD, at the closing of the 1980s, the regime cleared all influential Ogaadeen officers from sensitive positions in the army and one of their most senior officers, former Minister of Defence, General Adan Abdullahi Nuur "Gabyow" was sent to jail at the end of 1988

In reaction to General Gabyow's arrest, the Ogaadeen officers and their near kinsmen in the Absame clans (the Jidwaaq, Baalad, Weyteen) stationed in Hargeysa, in the north, mutinied. The group led by Colonel Ahmed Omar

---

32. John Markakis, National and Class Conflict, 1990, pp.228-231.

Jees, called themselves the National Army. Later, it moved to the south and in August 1989 it merged with the Somali Action Front (SAF), another Ogaadeen group led by Major Bashir Salaad "Bililiqo", formed in early 1989 in the southern part of Somalia. Together they formed the Somali Patriotic Front (SPM) and which soon confronted both the government forces and the Mareehaan militia funded by the regime.

In the opinion of Greenfield "with the Ogaadeen out of the MOD coalition, the regime's morale collapsed."[33] The regime's growing inventory of crises already included an economic malaise, which was compounded by the suspension of United States military and financial support in the late 1980s.

The End of Siyaad Barre's Rule

Sensing the SSDF and SNM threats to his rule and the breaking-up of the MOD, the General ignited his old tribal ploy by inciting the Daaroods, with a campaign secretly known as Daaroodiya, which aimed to unite the Daarood clans against the menace of the Isaaq (and later the Hawiye). The regime was set to play its last and habitual card, clan rivalry, by setting one against the other. The poem *"O Daarood, come together, now the disgrace has gone too far"*[34] did not have the impact that he expected — as Daaroods (i.e. the Majeerteen clan and later the Ogaadeen) were antagonised under his rule — and it could not revive the frail and dying MOD alliance.

---

33. Richard Greenfield, Somalia After the Fall, *Africa Report*, March-April 1991, p.18.
34. In Somali "Yaa Daarood ahay durugtay ceebtiiye".

In contrast, this provoked a corresponding affect with the Isaaqs and Hawiye joining in Irir solidarity.[35]

Barre skilfully manipulated the old feuds to his advantage. The Somali inter-clan conflict is centred on feuds, and it aims to injure or eliminate the hostile clan. The lost blood is generally added to the account of hereditary feuds, creating a perpetual conflict. Traditionally, the relationships between clans, lineages or other segments tended to be potentially hostile; one can therefore imagine what can happen when the state institutions are used to exploit this hostility. Barre's policy plunged the whole country into an explosive situation by such exploitation.

The Hawiye, who occupy the area around Muqdisho and the central rangelands, were until 1989 indolently acquiescent to the regime.[36] Barre avoided any confrontation with them by rewarding them for their passiveness. Since they were also subject to the changing situation, the dictator's relations with the Hawiye were thwarted by the formation in Rome of the United Somali Congress (USC) in 1989 by Hawiye politicians who had left the SNM and the SSDF.

Led by Ali Wardhigley, a former Information Minster of the civilian government, and Ali Hagarrey, the USC, which draws its support from the Hawiye clans of the Muqdisho suburbs and Central Somalia, remained a solely political organization until the end of 1989, when it was joined by General Mahamed Farah Garaad "Aydiid", who changed the organization into a fighting force. Mohamed Farah Aydiid

---

35. I M Lewis, The Death and Birth of the Somali State, p.7.
36. Said S. Samatar, *Somalia: A Nation In Turmoil*, A Minority Rights Group, August 1991, p.20.

was the Somali ambassador to India in the late 1980s, but had earlier been imprisoned for six years by Barre's regime. With the help of the SNM, Aydiid visited Ethiopia and gained support to organise and mobilise the Hawiye armed opposition.

To strengthen his position in Somalia, General Aydiid signed an agreement with the SNM and SPM on 2 October, 1990 in Dire Dawa.[1] Among other things, the agreement stipulated the joint effort of the three organizations, with the help of Ethiopia, to overthrow Siyaad Barre and then form a government afterwards.

However, General Aydiid's reorganisation clashed with the organization's founders in Rome, people such as Ali Wardhigley, the Secretary-General of the USC. On the other side of the conflict lay a traditional rivalry between the pastoral Habar Gidir clan (General Aydiid's kinsmen), who live mainly in central Somalia, and the mostly sedentary Abgaal/Murursade clans (Ali Wardhigley and Ali Hagarrey's clansmen). The USC leadership struggle was one of the main factors that generated the bitter war between the two groups in Muqdisho after General Siyaad Barre's fall in January 1991, catapulting Somalia into the world headlines as a human disaster of a scale not previously seen. (see below).

Adding to the list of the four armed opposition groups, the SSDF, SNM, SPM and USC, two more clan-based opposition groups were formed at the close of 1989. The Somali Democratic Alliance (SDA) of northern Somalia was founded in November 1989, by the Gadabuursi clan

---

1. Warmurtiyeed Wadajir Ah Oo Ay Soo Saareen SNM, USC & SPM, Somalia, 11/5/91.

(Dir clan family) against the Somali National Movement (Isaaq) militia. The Somali Democratic Movement (SDM) was established at the beginning of 1990 by the Rahanweyn clans of the Upper Jubba.

Unfortunately, the opposition movements were more clan affiliated than nationalistic, and the people became as much disappointed by these as by Barre's government. They were divided to such an extent that they were prolonging and perpetuating Barre's rule.[2] No opposition transcended traditional interests. As they applied the same political methods as that of Barre, the opposition movement became another way to further clan interests with arms.

Although most opposition groups rallied round a clan identity, the Islamic Party was in opposition to the regime on religious grounds. It was established after ten *culumos* (religious men) were publicly executed on 23 January, 1975. The *culumos* resisted a government decree of January 1975 that amended the Islamic law (Sharia Law) of inheritance by giving men and women equal rights under the Family Law (*Xeerka Qoyska*). The *culumos* accused the regime of attempting to distort *sura* Anisa (Women, IV) — and all matters related to civil status restricted by the Qoran and the Sunna — after General Siyaad Barre publicly asserted that certain verses of the Qoran were obsolete. Many religious leaders openly opposed his interpretation and during Friday sermons they criticised the General's new law. Within hours they were arrested by the National Security Service men and a few days later ten *culumos* were sentenced to death by firing squad by the National Security Court.

---

2. See "Divided They Stood", *African Events*, February 1991, p.24.

Aspiring to establish an Islamic state in Somalia, the Islamic group worked underground until 1986 when they again resurfaced and publicly denounced General Siyaad Barre's regime. The NSS rounded up their leaders and nine of them were given life imprisonment in 1987.

The Islamic group did not give up their political campaign. In fact, they rioted against the arrest of the Muqdisho mosque *imams* in July 1989. Consequently, more than one hundred were killed and wounded when the Red Berets, the dreaded presidential guards, were sent to contain the riot.

The State's Failure

Only at the end of 1989 did General Barre promise to introduce political reforms in the following year by amending the Constitution. However, this came too late, as in this period, owing to the civil war, Somalia was already in flames. These facts clearly showed the principle behaviour of the General which can be expressed in the French maxim *"Apres moi le deluge"*. To weaken his enemies, General Siyaad Barre had systematically incited one clan against another. Between 1980 and 1990 there was not a clan that did not fight against its neighbouring, and sometimes related, clans. The list is long: the Majeerteen fought against the Mareehaan, the Hawaadle (Hawiye) against the Ayr (Habar Gidir), the Leelkase against the Sa'ad (Habar Gidir), the Majeerteen against the Sa'ad (Habar Gidir), the Abgaal against the Hawaadle, the Mareehaan against the Saleebaan (Habar Gidir), the Dhulbahante (Daarood) against the Habar Tol-Je'le (Isaaq), the Ogaadeen against the Mareehaan, the Duduble (Habar

Gidir) against the Ayr (Habar Gidir), the Isaaq clans against the Gadabuursi (Dir), the Habar Yonis (Isaaq) against the Ogaadeen (Daarood), the Issa (Dir) against the Isaaq clans, the Galgale (Daarood)[3] against the Abgaal (Hawiye), the Sideedle against Sagaalle (both of the Rahanweyn clan-family).

A state is a carrier of a set of coercive and integrative functions executed by an array of institutions that can be called "government".[4] In contrast to what was supposed to be state responsibility, here was a regime whose policies contradicted the state's duties to maintain order.

To a Dead-End

Despite sensing his doom, Barre was supremely concerned with his survivability without making the necessary changes. After two decades of oppressive policy, his very survival was in doubt. The senseless obstinacy with which Barre was trying to hang on against all odds was leading the Somali state to a dead end. As he suffocated all attempts at peaceful change or reform, the only result which could develop was a violent breakdown of polity.

The uncompromising attitudes which Barre's regime firmly held contributed to the coming of the extremists, known as warlords, whose solution was to resort to force to solve Somalia's plight. Coupled with a divided opposition, the situation was really explosive.

At the close of the decade, more regions were slipping out of the control of the regime. Only Muqdisho remained in

---
3. This group is believed to be part of the Majeerteen clan.
4. Moshe Lewin, *The Gorbachev Phenomenon*, 1988, p.7.

Siyaad Barre's hands and thus he earned the name "Mayor of Muqdisho".

Isolated and suspicious at this time, even of his own Mareehaan kinsmen, General Siyaad Barre tightened security around himself and his family by nominating his son, General Maslah Mahamed Siyaad, to lead a newly formed sector that was to guard Muqdisho in the desperate hope of saving his last stronghold there; and appointed his son-in-law, General Mahamed Said "Morgan", as his Defence Minister.

The new Defence Minster soon started major military operations, one of which was to clear the road between Muqdisho and Galkayo. The road, which connects the southern regions with central and northern Somalia, was swarming with both guerrillas and bandits. In spite of the operation's military success, it was to create animosity among the population as the troops pillaged, abused and sometimes killed the people (mainly Hawiye) who lived in the area, and who were suspected of being supporters of government opposition.

The operation was another classic example of the policy of the regime in action. The troops were now being projected as 'Daarood', and the tactic was to provoke the Hawiye and turn their anger towards the Daarood, with the aim of creating panic in the area. In reality, the troops were "soldiers of fortune" from different groups — lured by the looting — and, of course, from the regime's last diehards. The regime's strategy was partially achieved in that the Hawiye clans were inflamed. The attitude of the Daarood clans was more equivocal, but not without suspicion and distrust of the regime, born of past experience. Add to this the regime's own propaganda machine, and the tactics of certain of the Hawiye's prominent political figures (whose ambitions could find parallels with those of Barre as they sought to exploit the circumstances to their own advantage), the situation was charged with, hostility and all kinds of paranoia which could tear apart a society.

For the country this was a crucial time. It was on the brink of disintegration. In May 1990, one hundred and fourteen prominent politicians, some of them respected citizens from former civilian governments, intellectuals and traditional leaders, tried at the last hour to save the country. They proposed a platform for dialogue and reconciliation and a means by which an interim government could be formed to lead the country to free elections.[5] This group, known as the Manifesto Group, made up from a crosssection of Somali society, confronted the General with a list of solutions to salvage the country from the abyss; it suggested among other things that he resign and hand over power to a caretaker government.[6]

Instead, General Siyaad Barre stubbornly refused to give up and declared a state of emergency, putting the army on full alert, even though most of it had deserted. Most of the Manifesto Group were arrested and taken to court[7] and on the day of their trial, in January, the whole population

---

5. An Open Letter to President Mahamed Siyaad Barre, *Horn of Africa*, Vol. XIII, N°. 1&2, Jan-March & April-June 1990, pp.109-144.

6. Mahamed Osman Omar, *The Road to Zero: op. cit.*, pp.196-7.

7. An Open Letter to President Mahamed Siyaad Barre, *Horn of Africa*, Vol. XIII, N°. 1&2, Jan-March & April-June 1990, pp.109-119.

of Muqdisho came out in support of those prominent personalities.[8] They surrounded the court, asking for the release of the detainees. The pressure forced Barre to release them, but only to ruthlessly kill two of them, Haji Muse Boqor and Hashi Weheliye in January 1991.[9]

The Manifesto signatories had also proposed a meeting with the armed opposition to negotiate and thrash out a peaceful transition. However, the three allied armed factions (SNM, SPM and USC/Aydiid) refused. Behind their objections to accept the Manifesto as intermediary was a claim that some of the leading figures of the group were prominent personalities of the former civilian government. Another anxiety was that, having their own agendas, the three armed factions sought to press for military victory and not negotiation with Barre.

Many foreign residents and embassy staff began to depart, as the situation in the country was deteriorating, and as the rebel advance towards the last fortress of the despot got nearer day by day.

Although the hope of any reconciliation was slim, Italy and Egypt proposed two meetings between the regime and the rebel movements in Rome, but they did not materialise. They tried to arrange another, but again they failed.

To gain more time in the hope of averting his imminent collapse, on 25 December, General Siyaad Barre announced that he would introduce a multi-party system, with elections to be conducted in the coming February 1991. The following

---

8. See "Mogadishu Burning", *African Events,* February 1991, p.24.
9. Though there could be many reasons for Siyaad Barre to kill these prominent men, however, there is a rumour which believes that many other groups may have reason to eliminate the Manifesto Group.

week he appointed Omar Arte Qalib, a former Foreign Minster (1969-76) and long-term prisoner of the Barre regime, as Prime Minster.

Because of the brittleness of the security circumstances, the situation worsened when a group of armed men looted a store in the Wardhigley District of Muqdisho mainly inhabited by the Hawiye clans, the main supporters of the USC. The cries for help of the victims attracted many people, and they chased the ravagers. After a hot pursuit the culprits retreated into a camp which belonged to the Red Berets, bodyguards of the President.[10]

This event prompted an uprising in Wardhigley. Ironically, the Red Berets were sent in to suppress the uprising. To crush the riot, the Red Berets indiscriminately shelled the Wardhigley quarter, killing and wounding several hundred civilians, including children and women. Nevertheless, they could no longer control the growing riot which, by this time, was organized by USC officers.

Unable to overwhelm the uprising, which by this time had expanded to other parts of Muqdishu, Barre tried desperately to hang on until when he was forced to flee to his home region, Garbaharrey, in the Gedo Region in the south. By fleeing, however, he left behind a power vacuum which soon became a source of quarrels between the opposition groups.

The USC, whose support lived in the area surrounding the capital, became predominent, and on 27 January, 1991 overran the Presidential Palace to take control of Muqdisho.

---

10. Mahamed Abdulle Ibrahim, field note, interviewed on September 15, 1992, London, England.

Chapter VII

THE
DISINTEGRATION

Without consulting other opposition organizations, and without considering the political and social repercussions of not doing so, the USC leadership appointed Ali Mahdi Mahamed as interim president on 29 January, 1991.[1] Ali Mahdi was a former member of the elected civilian parliament, a wealthy hotelier and also a Manifesto Group member.

The unilateral decision was immediately interpreted as a Hawiye bid for power. Ironically, at the swearing in ceremony, Ali Mahdi was flanked by senior loyal officers of General Siyaad Barre. Among them were General Husein Kulmiye Afrah, former Second-Vice President and former senior

---

1. Ahmed I Samatar, The Curse of Allah", in *The Somali Challenge*, ed. Ahmed I. Samatar, 1994, pp. 95-133.

member of the Supreme Revolutionary Council,[2] Mahamed Sheikh Osman, long-time Finance Minster, and General Mahamed Jili-ow, commander of the National Security Service's regional office in the capital, where the loathsome underground prison known as Godka was situated.

In the meantime, the USC fighters began to carry out their reprisal against General Siyaad Barre's regime. But within a short time their operation degenerated into a witch-hunt against anybody whom they identified as Daarood, including those who were opposed to Barre's regime.[3] In the following months, thousands of Daarood civilians were indiscriminately killed,[4] their property looted, and Daarood women raped.[5] Thousands of Daarood families took refuge in Sheikh Ali Suufi mosque.[6] The most fortunate went under the protection of Hawiye relatives.

---

2. In Search of Stability, *African Events*, April 1991, p.10.

3. Amnesty International, *Somalia: A Human Rights Disaster*, Al-Index:AFR-52/01/92, August 1992, p.5. See Ahmed I Samatar, The Curse of Allah", in *The Somali Challenge,* ed. Ahmed I. Samatar, (Boulder, Colorado: Lynne Rienner Publishers, 1994), pp. 95-133. See also Mohammed-Abdi Mohammed, Autopsie de la crise, *Forum: La guerre civile en Somalie: Quand? Comment? Pourquoi?* 7 et 8 Avril 1992, p.33. Somaliland: Rising from the Ruins, *Horn of Africa Bulletin*, Vol.4 No.1, January-February 1992.

4. Mark Bradbury, "Extract of a Report to the Inter-NGO Committee for Somalia (U.K.)" *About Southern Somalia*, August 1991, p.2-3.

5. Amnesty International, *Somalia: A Human Rights Disaster*, Al-Index:AFR-52/01/92, August 1992, p.5. See also "Extract from a Report to the Inter-NGO Committee for Somalia (UK) About Southern Somalia" , Mr. Mark Bradbury, August 1991.

6. Extract from "Report About USC Dominated Southern Somalia in March 1991, Prepared by Inter-NGO Committee for Somalia".

In early July a Somali Airlines plane was hijacked whilst en route to Djibouti, and taken to Luuq (Lugh). The hijacker was identified as Daarood; in retaliation 150 Daarood in Muqdisho were rounded up and reportedly killed.[7]

The opposition campaigns, started by different Somali groups in the hope of toppling a dictatorial regime, had become distorted. Instead of the campaigns converging in a new nationalistic platform, faction leaders sought to use the support they had for their personal ambition, and at the cost of the people they claimed to represent. In the south the USC-Hawiye struggle against a regime became a struggle between Daarood — projected as being synonymous with the regime - and Hawiye. The fact that the first victims of the Barre regime had been from the Daarood clans, (e.g. the Majeerteen and Ogaadeen) was lost sight of.

Paradoxically, the UN and many aid agencies seemed little concerned about the scale of the atrocities. Why the UN and non-governmental organisations (NGOs) preferred to turn a blind eye to the human rights abuses is itself a matter of concern.

The UN and international aid agencies were concerned to avoid clashing with the dominant groups in a given area of their operations. In so doing, they chose to ignore the critical role that disregard for human rights had played in creating the 1991-2 famine. In their defence, however, those from the international community were under threat of being shot or beaten. They were also compelled to pay excessively for their

---

7. Ibid., p.2.

security.[8] Anyone attempting to break the 'law of silence' might expect to meet with a tragic end. This happened to Sean Devereaux, a British UNICEF worker, who was killed in Kismaayo when he revealed the news of the killing of more than 200 Harti men by militia loyal to Colonel Ahmed Omar Jees, on the nights between 8-10 December 1992. The memory of Sean Devereaux would thereafter linger in the minds of the aid workers.[9]

Within a few months of the collapse of the Barre regime, the Daaroods who for generations had inhabited Benaadir, the Lower Shabeelle, Upper Shabeelle, and the Lower Jubba and Bay regions were 'clan-cleansed' from the area.

Somalia was without the authority of a central government. Old hostilities could not be contained. It was the nightmare scenario posited by the political historian Hobbes come true: circumstances where, without intervention people would conduct a 'war of all against all'.

The 'clan cleansing' in 1991 seemed like an acting out of an old Abgaal *shirib* (improvised song and dance) from the 1940s:

Doon raacdaa ama dabaalataa, Daarood dalkayga iiga guur.
Either by boat or by swimming, O Daarood, leave my country.

---

8. Julian Ozanne, Somali Gunmen Hold Aid Agencies to Ransom as Thousands Starve to Death, *Financial Times*, 6 November 1992.
9. Human Rights Watch/Africa, Somalia Faces the Future: Human Rights in a Fragmented Society, Vol.7, No.2, April 1995, p.22.

Power Struggle Within the USC

The hurried nomination of Ali Mahdi Mahamed to the presidency was challenged by other Hawiye leaders, particularly by the ambitious General Mahamed Farah Aydiid, the USC force commander, who was then outside Muqdisho. General Aydiid demanded the presidency for himself since he was the one who led the USC fighters against General Siyaad Barre's regime, a claim that was fiercely rejected by Ali Mahdi.[10]

Trouble was in the making as the two Hawiye strongmen from different sub-clans headed for a clash. The root cause behind the two men's conflict lay in their traditional clan rivalry. Ali Mahdi's Abgaal clan, who led a mainly settled life, were dominant in the area surrounding the north of Muqdisho, while General Aydiid's Habar Gidir lived in the central regions and led a nomadic life. The ascendancy to power of Ali Mahdi (Abgaal) reflected the fear of the settled people threatened by pastoral domination.

As the atmosphere was charged with tension, Ali Mahdi called a national conference to convene in Muqdisho. But his call fell on deaf ears, since the rebel groups were angry over his hasty decision to claim power. Moreover, the leadership crisis within the USC led each Hawiye group to lay claim to a different part of Muqdisho. Soon the capital became divided between the different Hawiye groups. The condition deteriorated into anarchy where the rule of the gun became law. The high-powered weapons obtained by General Siyaad Barre's regime, first from the Soviet Union then from the

---

10. Ahmed I Samatar, The Curse of Allah", in *The Somali Challenge*, ed. Ahmed I. Samatar, 1994, pp. 95-133.

US, and later from Libya, Germany, China and Italy fell into the hands of these groups. Again the situation was exacerbated when new Libyan and Sudanese weapons arrived in Muqdisho during this period.

The Clash of the Opposition Groups

Whereas the USC was divided over Muqdisho they were united in their efforts to overrun the Somali Patriotic Movement (SPM) which was positioned outside Muqdisho, near Afgooye. The USC inflicting heavy casualties on the SPM, pushing them on to Jilib and Jamame near Kismaayo, 500 kilometres south of the capital.

When General Siyaad Barre fled Muqdisho, he retreated to his home country in the Gedo region of southern Somalia. From this new headquarters he planned to take back Muqdisho. However, he could not muster the confidence of the politically divided Daaroods, many of whom had been vicitms of the indiscriminate attacks of the USC and who now blamed Siad for their anguish.

For the ousted dictator, leaving Muqdisho was a manoeuvre intended to be temporary. He tried to exploit the fear and anger of the Daaroods, but he misjudged that anger, which was greater towards him than towards the USC.

To defend themselves, Daaroods who had fled from the capital regrouped in Kismaayo and attempted to form a united front. In mid-February 1991, they formed the Somali National Front (SNF) with twenty-one executive men. At the end of the month, under the command of General Husein Hassan, they launched a massive offensive against the USC, and nearly reached Muqdisho. However, in the eleventh hour the coalition of Daaroods suffered a catastrophic setback when the militia loyal to Barre, after reaching the vicinity of the capital, started to display placards showing Barre's pictures. The Daarood coalition under the banner of SNF, already debilitated, now dissipated very quickly. It could not stand against the fierce counter attack of the better organised USC forces which drove them far out of Muqdisho, and without much resistance pursued them to the port of Kismaayo, capturing it on 23 April.

On 31 March, 1991, General Mahamed Farah Aydiid's faction of the USC reported, in a military communiqué, the beginning of a large scale offensive against the Mudug and Magertenia (former name of the Bari and Nugaal regions). In the following days they attacked Galkayo, the capital of the Mudug Region, killing and wounding 970 people.[11] Although the authenticity of the communiqué cannot be verified, the killings in Galkayo, the cradle of resistance to General Siyaad Barre in the central regions,[12] have been confirmed by Amnesty International[13] and foreign observers who visited the area.[14]

These confrontations were interpreted as Hawiye-Daarood clashes in the south (USC-SPM) and in the central regions

---

11. "Galkayo Falls into the USC Hand", *USC Military Communiqué*, Ref. No. USC/- DD/3/3/91, March 3, 1991.
12. "In Search of Stability", *African Events*, April 1991, p.10.
13. Amnesty International, *Somalia: A Human Rights Disaster*, Al-Index:AFR- 52/01/92, August 1992, p.6.
14. Mark Bradbury and Rick Davies, "A Report of the Assessment Mission to Bari, Nugaal, and Mudug Regions of Somalia from September 17th to September 30th to the Inter-NGO Committee for Somalia (UK)," October 1991, pp.56-8.

(SSDF-USC), and for some time detracted from the factional clashes within the USC.

While the south waged a war of attrition, the north was relatively calm. Using as a pretext the USC's unilateral decision to form a provisional government without consultation with the opposition, the SNM, which took control of the North-West and Tog-dheer regions, refused to attend the call by Ali Mahdi for a national conference on 28 February in Muqdisho.[15] Accordingly, on 18 May, 1991, approximately four months after Siyaad Barre's regime was ousted, the SNM declared the regions (what had constituted former British Somaliland), an independent Somaliland Republic. Their leaders took the stance that they had to concede to the 'pressure of their people'.[16] The SNM argued that its action was not secessionist but rather the reinstatement of the status which existed for four days, 26-30 June 1960, before British and Italian Somalilands were united into the Republic of Somalia. This unilateral decision, however, complicated the Somali dilemma and further distanced the glimmer of hope for a conclusion to the Somali plight. It raised new concerns, not least whether this would now signal the end of the long road to pan-Somalism and the unity of the Somali nation. Despite the breakdown of the Somali state, the notion of a unitary Somali nation could not consciously be easily let go of.

Whatever reasons the SNM gave for its declaration of secession, however, most non-Isaaq people living in the north

---

15. Jean Hélène, "Le clan Nordiste des Isak choisit de faire cavalier seul", *Le Monde,* March 1, 1991.
16. John Drysdale, Proud Northers Seek to Stand Alone, *New African,* Tuesday, June 25, 1991.

were uneasy, and suspected that it was an attempt at 'Isaaq hegemony'. Given the clan hostility and feuds in the north in the days of Barre and the subsequent collapse of state institutions, this was a recipe for fear and anxiety among substantial groups of the population in the north.

The Djibouti Conference

While the future of Somalia looked more and more grim, the first preparation for a conference of national reconciliation took place when former President Adan Abdulle Osman (1960-67) and former Prime Ministers Abdirisaq Haji Husein (1964-67) and Mahamed Haji Ibrahim Igal (1967-69) met in Djibouti. Under the auspices of Djibouti's President Hassan Guleed Abtidon, the representatives of the SSDF, SPM, USC and SDM met in Djibouti from 5 to 11 June, 1991. However, the SNM refused to attend the meeting.

Between 15 July and 21 July a second national reconciliation conference was held in Djibouti and this time only two more groups, the United Somali Front (USF)[17] and the Somali Democratic Alliance (SDA), joined. Again, the SNM, now the Somaliland Republic, declined to attend the peace conference. Out of eleven opposition groups in this period, only seven were present at the peace conference. International observers also took part.[18]

---

17. United Somali Front (USF) is a Ciise-based group and was formed in response to the SNM-dominated Isaaq in the north. The six opposition groups which attended the conference where as following: the SPM, SSDF, USC, SDA, SDM and USF.

18. The international observers which took part in the Second Djibouti reconciliation conference of 5-11 June 1991: USA, Italy, Egypt, France, Germany, Nigeria, Ethiopia, Saudi Arabia, Libya,

The conference recommended:
1. the implementation of a ceasefire from Friday 26 July 1991.
2. that the unity of Somalia be sacrosanct, therefore the provisional government that would be formed would be mandated to enforce the unity of the country and the people.
3. adherence to the 1960 constitution for a period of up to two years from the day when the new government was formed.
4. the formation of a government involving the opposition groups.
5. establishment of a legislature of 123 members based on the eight regional administrative areas of the civilian government before 1969.
6. the enactment of regional autonomy.

The Somali people longed for peace after two decades of military dictatorship and the chaos that followed its demise regime. However, the conference failed to address the real issue and the root cause of the chaos, and instead endorsed Ali Mahdi Mahamed, who was part of the problem, as interim president for two years.

Yemen, Kenya, Uganda, Sudan, Oman, the USSR, the Arab League, the Organisation of African Unity (OAU), the Organisation of Islamic Countries (OIC), the European Community (EC) and the Inter-Governmental Authority for Drought and Development (IGADD). See Shirwaynaha Dib-u-Heshiisiinta Shacbiga Soomaaliyeed Oo Ay ka soo Qaybgaleen Jabhadaha SSDF, SPM, USC, SDM, SDA iyo USF, Djibouti 15-21 Luulyo 1991.

The congress fell short of overall national expectations as the country was fragmented into clan-held or clan controlled regions. It was unrealistic that some of the prominent clan groups were denied participation in the reconciliation process. This was also infringing the customary Somali way of settling conflicts. Upholding of the principle of fair representation and the participation of all clans were supposed to be the very basis of the conference.

Unfortunately, this did not become the case. On the contrary, by giving credibility to the undemocratic developments perplexing the country, the Djibouti resolutions had more negative than positive results, and ignited new inter-clan hostilities, mainly within the Hawiye and between them and the Daarood.[19]

The Muqdisho Clash

In Muqdisho, the reconfirmation of Ali Mahdi Mahamed as interim president triggered, on 6 July, 1991, a bloody confrontation between Ali Mahdi's Abgaal clan and that of the USC Chairman, General Mahamed Farah Aydiid's Habar Gidir clan, both from the Hawiye group. More than three hundred people died and almost five hundred were wounded. After elders of other Hawiye clans pleaded with the warring clans to stop the fighting, the violence was halted.

In October, Ali Mahdi announced his government of seventy-two ministers and vice ministers, based upon all signatory parties to the Djibouti conference. He gave the

---

19. Mahamed Ali Direh, The Process of Restoring Peace and National Reconciliation in Somalia: A Handbook for Inter-Clan Dialogue, 1/4/92, p.25

premiership to Omar Arte Qalib (Isaaq), former Premier of Siyaad Barre's last days. Now General Aydiid, who longed only for the presidency, had reason to fight as his group was excluded from the power sharing.

In the meantime, the city was gripped by anarchy and food and essential commodities became scarce. On 15 November the two sides again clashed, but this time the situation was out of the control of the elders, and indiscriminate shelling was used by both sides.[20] The situation deteriorated. As an observer described it, "the smell of blood and decay is everywhere."[21]

Fighting between these two groups caused an already fragile situation to deteriorate. Consequently, famine worsened as a direct consequence of fighting and "every aspect of government and organisation in Somalia" was destroyed.[22] By this time any hope of resuscitation of the state was remote.

In the Height of the Famine

Because of the outbreak of the civil war and subsequent anarchy in Somalia, many minority groups were uprooted and forced to flee the country. Among them there were the Wambalazi (Reer Barawe), the Reer Hamar (Gibil-ad), and the Bajun. Barawa became transformed into a battleground between the USC and SNF initially, and between the SNA and SPM later on. From February 1991 to May 1992 Barawa

---

20. Amnesty International, *Somalia: A Human Rights Disaster*, Al-Index:AFR- 52/01/92, August 1992, p.2.
21. Mogadishu in Blood, *Horn of African Bulletin*, January-February 1992.
22. Starved of Hope, *The Guardian*, 15th September 1992.

changed hands nine times between these groups as it fell victim both to the atrocities of the freelance bandits (locally known as *mooryaan, jirri* or *day-day*) and those of the warring factions.[1] The anguish and suffering of this community is depicted in the words of - Abubakar Dheere "Abuu Dheere":[2]

> If this group comes, the other group leaves.
> They loot and take away everything.
> I cannot distinguish among the ants,
> for the colour is the same.

After the retreat to his home region of Gedo, in the southern part of Somalia, Barre's militia took control of a vast area of the adjacent regions, especially the Bay region, which was mainly inhabited by the Rahanweyn and Bantu people. Barre's forces fed on the grain reserves (bakaaro), livestock and water reserves of these people, whose main activity was agriculture. A man-made famine was thus in the making. And it was being assisted by a number of other factors, namely, (i) the fighting between the SNA and Barre's loyal forces, (ii) the split within the Somali Democratic Movement — a Rahanweyn based organisation —which sparked confrontation within the Rahanweyn, (iii) the fighting in Muqdisho which first concealed the news of the famine, and later hampered international efforts to help the affected people, and (iv) banditry and looting of food intended for the famine victims.

---

1. Ken Menkhaus, "Statement Regarding the Status of the Barawan (Bravan) People of Coastal Southern Somalia," May 3, 1993.
2. Lee V Cassanelli and Bana M S Banafunzi, "A Recent Poetic Lament from Brava", 199?.

It was only when Baydhaba (Baidoa) hit the international media as the "City of Death" that the world realised the severity of the situation. For thousands of people this was too late. Though this part of Somalia was the most severely hit area, other parts of the country were hardly better off.

The Somaliland Republic

The only clan-family that appeared united was the Isaaq, but the situation changed in mid-December 1991 when tension increased within the SNM. The controversy developed when the self-proclaimed Somaliland Republic tried to establish an inter-clan force without a territorial basis.

During the struggle, the SNM was divided into guerrilla groups on a regional basis.[3] During the final integration process, differences appeared between the Defence Minister, Colonel Mahamed Kahin Ahmed (Habar Tol-Je'le, Isaaq), and the president, Abdirahman Ahmed Ali "Tuur" (Habar Yonis, Isaaq). The controversy induced the self-proclaimed Republic's President to replace his defence minister.[4] In January 1992, fighting erupted between the Habar Tol-Jecle and the Habar Yoonis in Bur-o (Bura-o), 150 kilometres south-west of Berbera, killing many,[5] and leading to a flow of refugees who fled the town.[6]

---

3. "A Clan Integrated Army", *Horn of Africa Bulletin*, January-February 1992, p.3.
4. Ibid., p.3.
5. Amnesty International, *Somalia: A Human Rights Disaster*, Al-Index:AFR- 52/01/92, August 1992, p.7.
6. Fighting in Bura-o, *Horn of Africa Bulletin*, January-February 1992.

Amid the instability, a conference, in session since 24 January, 1993, and held by the Somaliland community elders was concluded in Boorame (Borame) in May 1993. It reached two main resolutions: (1) the need for a country-wide security framework, and (2) the establishment of a national organisational structure. At the same meeting, the elders elected Mahamed Haji Ibrahim Igal, a former prime minister (1967-1969), as President of Somaliland, and Colonel Abdirahman Aw-Ali Farah as Vice-President.

The North-Eastern Region (NER)

The North-Eastern Region (NER) on the whole enjoyed relative peace and stability. This was with the exception of the Mudug area, where clashes between the USC — Aydiid faction —and the SSDF/SNDU[7] were centred.

On 21 December, 1991, the traditional religious leaders, intellectuals and politicians of the north-eastern regions - the Bari, Nugaal, part of the Mudug and part of the Galguduud[8] - agreed to form a regional administration under the leadership of former Police Chief (1960-1969), General Mahamed Abshir Muse, with Boqor Abdullahi Boqor Muse as General Coordinator.

The SSDF leadership that controlled the North-Eastern Region (NER), justified their move because of the collapse of the central government and the need to create self-reliance and

---

7. SNDU (Somali National Democratic Union) is an opposition movement mainly supported by the Leelkase clan (Daarood). It controls part of Mudug region.
8. "Dowlad Goboleed Lagu Dhawaaqay", *Himilo*, Cadadka 22aad, Garoowe, 3 Janaayo 1992, p.2.

self-defence. However, their stability was seriously threatened and nearly crumbled when a Muslim fundamentalist group calling itself *Ittixaad Al-Islaami* (Islam Unity) attempted to take control of the North-Eastern Region in the early morning of 19 June, 1992. The Ittixaad Al-Islaami's attempt to overpower the North-Eastern Region's control reflected a well-coordinated plan by fundamentalist groups whose objective was to fill in the power vacuum in Somalia.[9] The group was funded from abroad, and had been extending their influence across the Somali-populated area of the Horn of Africa to establish a stronghold for militant Islam in the region.[10]

However, the SSDF military commander, Colonel Abdullahi Yusuf Ahmed struck before the Islamic militants could secure the region. In the resulting fighting between the well armed and better organized Ittixaad Al-Islaami force on one hand and the SSDF force on the other, more than two hundred people perished and many more were wounded. The Islamic fundamentalists retreated into the mountainous area of the Sanag region.

The Kismaayo Conflict

After the collapse of the Somali national unitary state no clan-family was free from conflict. On many occasions fighting broke out amongst all clans, except the Digil.

The Daaroods' confrontation was centred on Kismaayo, the regional capital of the Lower Jubba region, where the

---

9. *Maktabka Jihaadka,* 25.10.1412 (Hijra).
10. Jennifer Parmelee, Somalia What Remains, *International Herald Tribune,* 12th November 1992.

main contenders were the Harti and Mahamed Subeer of the Ogaadeen clan, both of whom are from the Daarood clan-family. Their continued clashes resulted in death and starvation for many innocent civilians, in the now all too familiar pattern which had repeated itself the length and breadth of Somalia in the current period.

This was not the first time in its history that Kismaayo had been at the centre of strife. For centuries Somali clans migrated, first from south-eastern Ethiopia, which is believed to be the cradle of their earliest ancestors,[11] spreading north-eastward to populate the Horn. Centuries later a new wave of migration[12] began flowing in the opposite direction, to the south and west. The traditional migration patterns that can be discerned show that the Somali clans followed two main routes: the river Shabeelle valley and along the line of coastal wells on the Indian Ocean littoral.[13]

By the close of the seventeenth century the Isaaq, Daarood, and Dir migrations had spread to much of the northern part of what is the Western Somaliland, and the southern part of the Jubba river up to the Tana river, presently Kenya.

The Daarood clans arrived in the inter-riverine land from the west late in the nineteenth century. However, they were forced to migrate further south up to the Jubba river area, by the Rahanweyn and Digil clans.

The Harti clans settled in coastal towns such as Kismaayo, where many of them had come by sea, as they had for centuries

---

11. Abdirahman Ali Hersi, *The Arab Factor in Somali History, op. cit.*, p.23.
12. Ibid., pp.25-26.
13. I M Lewis, Understanding Somalia, *op. cit.*, pp.1-2.

been conducting commercial activities along the coast.[14] The Mahamed Subeer clan settled inland from the coast, as far south as the Tana River on the Kenya border. Their neighbours to the northe were other Daarood clans, the Awlyahan of Ogaadeen and the Mareehaan, The Harti and Mahamed Subeer clans had never lived peacefully together, and towards the end of the nineteenth century the conflict between these two clans received the attention of Boqor Osman of the Sultanate of Majeerteen, when the Hartis were defeated by Mahamed Subeer in a battleground known today as Lafaha Ragga (also known as Lafa Harti Jaha),[15] near Kismaayo.

Towards the end of the nineteenth century, the British convinced Sayid Khalifa, Sultan of Zanzibar, to accept British management of the land under his suzerainty. This enabled the British to take control of these parts of the Somali-inhabited area. However, in 1905 they leased to the Italians the Benaadir coast which included Muqdisho, Marka (Merca), Barawa and Warsheikh. Furthermore, on 15 July, 1923 they ceded the Jubbaland[16] to Italian control under Corroli Zoli, the High Commissioner for the new territory of the Oltre Giuba.[17]

By the time Commissioner Zoli took control of the new territory (he had been sidetracked by the Harti and Mahamed Subeer) rumours had spread among the inhabitants that

---

14. Baashi Axmed Sahal, interview on 2 September 1993, in London, England.
15. Ibid.,
16. The Trans-Jubba area, from the Jubba's west bank to the Kenyan border.
17. Robert L Hess, *Italian Colonialism in Somalia, op. cit.*, pp.154-58.

the Italians favoured the Mahamed Subeer.[18] To quash this rumour and to convince the Somalis of "Italian impartiality", on 24 October, 1925, Zoli successfully concluded a peace settlement between the two warring clans[19] and placed as a buffer between them the Warday clan, an Oromo ethnic group.[20]

With the coming of Barre's regime in the 1970s, Kismaayo became a very important training centre, attracting thousands of young Ogaadeens. The government policy of rewarding certain sub-clans for their loyalty to the "Blessed Revolution", and the persecution of others for their rebellious tendency,[21] caused many Harti businessmen, especially the Majeerteen who were persecuted by the regime, to flee from Kismaayo.

In the wake of the civil war in Somalia in 1991, the Daaroods who fled the massacre of Muqdisho organised themselves in Kismaayo to become the Somali National Front. However, soon the SNF changed itself into a Mareehaan organization and the non-Mareehaan Daaroods were forced to organise themselves under the Somali Patriotic Movement, which had operated in this area since 1989. This decision caused a split within the SPM in December 1991, with one group, led by Colonel Ahmed Omar Jees, joining General Mahamed Farah Aydiid's SNA,[22] and the other group, commanded by former

---

18. Ibid, p.159.
19. Ibid, p.159.
20. Baashi Axmed Sahal, interviewed on 2 September 1993, London, England.
21. Siciid Faarax Maxamuud, Prisoners of Siyadist Culture, *Hal-Abuur*, Vol I, No. 1, Summer 1993, p.16.
22. Formed in October 1992, the Somali National Alliance is an alliance of four factions: USC (General Aydiid's faction), Somali

defence minister General Adan Abdullahi Nuur "Gabyow", bringing under its umbrella the Daarood clans.

While there was still disagreement among the Daaroods, on 23 April, 1991, the USC captured the port city which remained under their control until mid-July when the SPM, General Adan Abdullahi's faction, recaptured the town. Nevertheless, in May 1992, again Kismaayo came under the control of Colonel Jees's faction and his alliance, the Somali National Alliance.

To consolidate his power and cleanse his rival clan which was deeply rooted in the port city, Colonel Jees's loyal militia rounded up more than 200 of the best-educated businessmen, and traditional and religious leaders of the Harti clan shortly before the arrival of the US and Belgium forces in Kismaayo, for a mass execution on the nights between 8-10 December.[23]

In early March of the following year the control of the town again switched to General Adan Abdullahi and General Mahamed Said Hersi "Morgan", (the SPM military commander), whose supporters infiltrated the town and then attacked Colonel Jees's position by surprise.[24]

At the end of June 1993 a peace agreement was signed between the warring groups in which 152 delegates took

---

Democratic Movement (Mahamed Nur Aliyow's faction), Southern Somali National Movement, and SPM (Mahamed Omar Jees's faction).

23. Jane Perlez, Somali Killed 100 as US Troops Landed, *International Herald Tribune*, Tuesday, December 29, 1992, p.4. See also Mass Executions in Kismaayo, Somalia: A Case for Inquiry and Intervention, by Waruhiu & Muite, Nairobi, Kenya, January 8, 1993.
24. Mark Huband, Somalia Women Wage War in Town Split by Terrorism, *The Monitor*, March 23, 1993, p.12.

part as well as 50 observers.[25] The Jubbaland[26] community agreed to settle their differences peacefully and to create a suitable environment for coexistence. To achieve this goal they agreed to establish committees to supervise, (1) cease-fire and disarmament, (2) reconciliation of Jubbaland people, (3) travel and movement, and (4) restoration of property.

Barre's Last Bid

The ousted dictator Barre had remained in his home region of Gedo since his downfall. In April 1992, in the hope of regaining Muqdisho, he deployed his forces, now only his clansmen near Afgooye, 30 kilometres south of Muqdisho.

But the plan to deploy the Mareehaan militia outside their home region was objected to by some of his generals. A break-up of the Barre force's chain of command was sensed by the Somali National Alliance, which did not fail to take advantage of this golden opportunity. Within less than a week the SNA, without much resistance, pushed Barre out of the country. In pursuit, the SNA militia systematically rounded up members of the Mareehaan civilians (and anyone they identified as Daarood), and subjected them to mass torture, mutilation and execution.[27]

---

25. "The Jubbaland Peace Conference (Kismayo)", p.1.
26. Jubbaland is composed of three regions: Lower Jubba (Kismaayo), Middle Jubba (Bu'-aale) and Gedo (Garbaharrey).
27. Julian Ozanne, Somali Gunmen Hold Aid Agencies to Ransom as Thousands Starve to Death, *Financial Times,* 6 November 1992.

Chapter VIII

THE UN INVOLVEMENT

Because of lack of security, food could not reach the needy as food convoys were looted and ships were being shelled to turn them away. Furthermore, relief workers were threatened by armed gangs. Without the slightest moral standards, mafia-like groups imposed exorbitant fees on the UN and relief agencies to make them pay for their security.[28] The situation was desperate, as Mr Mike Whitlam, the British Red Cross Director-General, observed:

> I have never seen so many people in one place starving and dying... The smell of death and of the feeding kitchens is a combination I will not forget. The other

---

28. Julian Ozanne, Somali Gunmen Hold Aid Agencies to Ransom as Thousands Starve to Death, *Financial Times*, 6 November 1992.

feeling is of sheer frustration at trying to get food into place and being prevented by conflict from delivering it to the starving.[29]

The perpetual fighting in Somalia could not be ended without the involvement of the world community. However, UN officials insisted that they could not deploy any peace-keeping force without the consent of the warring parties; to do so would constitute a "breach of sovereignty". For how long should the integrity of a "disintegrated" sovereign state be safeguarded when thousands starved to death while millions were forced to flee the country or to live miserable lives in wretched huts, deprived of food, water, medicine, schooling, and even their pride as human beings?[30] Surprisingly, in mid-October 1992, the UN (Security Council Resolution 751 of 27 July 1992) reached agreement with the Muqdisho factions for 500 armed troops to guard Muqdisho port and airport and escort food convoys.[31] And on 28 October the United Nations Security Council passed a resolution ordering a further 3000 Blue Helmets to reinforce UNOSOM force in Somalia.

Operation Restore Hope?

Although the UN Secretary-General, Dr Boutros Boutros-Ghali, tried his best to shift the Security Council's attention, which was focused then on the Balkan war, to the plight of

---

29. A Far Cry from The Weary Front, *The Guardian*, 15th September 1992.

30. Operation Restore Hope?, *Horn of Africa Bulletin*, Vol.4, No. 6, November- December 1992.

31. Mark Huband, UN Troops Move into Mogadishu, *The Guardian*, September 14, 1992.

Somalia,[32] the United Nation agencies abandoned Somalia at a time when it was evident that a major famine was building up and people were dying in large numbers. This matter of the UN failure prompted Mahamed Sahnoun, the UN Special Representative for Somalia, who had been partially successful in his contact with some of the Somali parties, to criticise the UN policy and subsequently he was forced to resign.

Following the end of the Cold War, the UN had to shift its focus, and the Somali case was to become its first direct attempt at enforcing peace. It was a chance to prove that in a new world order, the UN could take effective military action.

Things were getting worse especially in the southern part of the country. As Somalia was being ripped apart by warlords who vied for power, the world community was less than interested in being involved in this war-torn country.

So it was that the Bush administration's announcement, on 20 November, 1992, to send 30,000 US troops as a humanitarian mission to Somalia,[33] surprised everybody. The US government, which had previously been blamed for objecting to any assistance to Somalia except humanitarian aid,[34] insisted on the operation and defined its objectives in the UN Security Council resolution 794. It was to be called Operation Restore Hope, and was to be under an American commander.

This sudden change of heart by the US government created suspicion. There was a feeling that it was meant to have political

---

32. "Poor Man's War" Unveiled, *West Africa*, 17-23 August 1992.
33. Martin Walker, 30.000 US troops Get Aid Role, *The Guardian*, 27th November 1992.
34. "While the World Hesitate", *The Guardian*, 15th September 1992. See Rakiya Omaar, Somalia's Nightmare, *West Africa*, 17-23 1993.

impact back home rather than help Somalia out of the abyss of despair. Indeed, this became clear when the special envoy of President George Bush, Mr Robert B. Oakley, preceded the US troops (under the UN International Task Force) to pave the way for Operation Restore Hope. To ensure a "smooth" arrival for the US troops, he bargained with General Aydiid and Ali Mahdi, the two warlords believed most responsible for the famine and the subsequent death of 350,000 people, and which had made Somalia, in the words of former UN Secretary-General Javier Peres De Cuellar, "the world's worst humanitarian disaster". The ambassador's political approach was interpreted by the warlords as the legitimisation of their authority, and was to affect and undermine the UN's own programme for dealing with the problem.

The Addis Ababa Peace Conference

Without political reconciliation the cycle of violence and death, from rape, starvation, destruction, and genocidee could not be brought to an end. Hoping to ease the situation, the UN organised a preparatory meeting in the Ethiopian capital on 4 January, 1993 which paved the way for the mid-March 1993 national reconciliation conference in the Africa Hall, Addis Ababa between 15 armed political groups[35]. The self-proclaimed Somaliland Republic took part as observers.

---

35. These were in two groups: (1) USC (Aydid), SPM (Omar Jees), SDM (Aliyow) and SSNM which attended as SNA coalition. (2) SSDF, USC (Ali Mahdi), SDA, SAMO, SNDU, SNF, SPM (Adan Abdullahi "Gabyow"), SNU, USF, USP and SDM (Abdulqadir Zoppe). This last group is known as Somali Salvation Alliance (SSA).

After chaotic negotiations an accord was finally arranged to halt hostility, to build the foundations for peace, to reconstruct and to rehabilitate Somalia.[36] The agreement stipulated, among other things, (1) disarmament and security, (2) rehabilitation and reconstruction, (3) the restoration of property and settlement of disputes, and (4) the creation of a transitional mechanism to become the political and legislative authority of Somalia for an interim period of two years.

This transitional mechanism was composed of four basic administrative levels:

1. the Transitional National Council (TNC) composed of 74- members, being (a) three representatives from each of the 18 regions, (b) five additional seats for Muqdisho, and (c) one nominee from each of the political factions.
2. the Central Administration Departments (CADs) responsible for national public administration.
3. the Regional Council (RCs) responsible for regional administration.
4. the District Council (DCs) responsible for the district affairs.

In spite that the US-led multinational forces from 30 countries (UNITAF) set task was left unfinished, i.e. the disarming of the warring factions, nevertheless, it helped to ease temporarily the famine.

Everything appeared to be going as planned when, on 3rd May, control was handed to the UN troops under a retired American Admiral, Jonathan Howe, designated UN

---

36. Addis Ababa Agreement of the First Session of the Conference on National Reconciliation in Somalia, 27th March 1993.

representative, and the Turkish, General Cevik Bir, the UN troop commander under the banner of UNOSOM II (Security Council Resolution 814). The UN troops at this time had been given the role of peace enforcement under the "enforcement provisions" of Chapter VII of the UN Charter which called for "further use of force to maintain peace throughout this fractious country and the disarming and demobilization of all armed groups."[37] Dr. Boutros-Ghali emphasised the matter in this way:

> There is no alternative but to resort to Chapter VII of the Charter... Experience has shown that this cannot be achieved by a UN operation based on the accepted principle of peacemaking.[38]

With the new mandate under Chapter VII, the UNOSOM's role changed from mediator to player and this in turn set the scene for confrontation.

When the time came to implement the Addis Ababa peace agreements, events suddenly took a drastic turn. On 5 June, Pakistani UN soldiers on a routine arms inspection near Radio Muqdisho (controlled by General Aydiid's militia), were ambushed, and 24 of them were killed. In the retaliatory fighting, 75 Aydiid supporters were killed and 350 wounded. In response to the attack on the Blue Helmets, the Security Council passed a resolution (No. 837) calling

---

37. James Bone, UN Prepares to Assume Sole Charge of Governing Somalia, *The Times*, 5th March 1993.
38. Martin Walker, UN Chief Urges Force to Help Somalia, *The Guardian*, December 1, 1192.

for the punishment of those responsible for the killing.[39] Aydiid was declared a wanted man, and was forced to hide for three months, during a UNOSOM II hunt which was eventually called off.

In a desperate attempt to neutralise General Aydiid's power base, UNOSOM II started to unleash its fire power to destroy the warlord's military stronghold. In the ensuing operation, they killed hundreds of innocent civilians. The death and destruction caused by the helicopter gunships and, in particular the highly sophisticated AC130s with their 105mm guns, created widespread Somali causalities, exposing UNOSOM's lack of preparedness in such a situation. As a consequence of this policy, however, General Aydiid was put in a stronger position than before. But the policy also created a split between the member states taking part in the operation — Italy, a former colonial power of Somalia, did its best to undermine the UN and the US operations — and left the UN's most ambitious peacekeeping mission ever in total disarray.

From this time the fate of the UN's post-Cold War order was evident as it "clearly contributed to its own demise in Somalia with shortsighted political strategies" and a distressing lack of responsibility and bureaucratic operation in the field.[40] This was also a lost of opportunity for the UN to help the Somalis who initially trusted the UN and placed too much

---

39. Making Monkeys of the UN, *The Economist*, July 10, 1993, p.60.
40. Ken Menkhaus, Understanding the UN's Failure in Somalia, *Life and Peace Review*, Life and Peace Institute, Vol. 8, Number 4, 1994, p.25.

reliance, to a degree of total dependence, on UNOSOM that it would solve all the Somali ills.

After the incident an enquiry led by Professor Tom Farer of the American University, concluded that "the claim that Aidid [Aydiid] authorised the SNA forces' attack on Pakistani forces is supported by clear and convincing evidence". He added that the attack was in violation of the 1962 Penal Code (still in force) and violated international law.[41]

UNOSOM's Failure of The Victims of War

Under Chapter VII of the United Nations, UNOSOM was to become the *de facto* government of Somalia from December 1992 to the end of March 1995. But it was to leave without achieving any progress on the humanitarian, political, security and economic fronts, and it "utterly fail[ed] in its mandate to make peace, to effect political reconciliation among the Somalis and restore national socio-economic institutions."[42]

Instead of concentrating their effort to help Somalis sort out their political differences, it seemed that UNOSOM only served to aggravate the complexities of the Somali conflict. UNOSOM's myopic and blinkered policy resulted in the pursuit of negative political trends, illustrated, for example, by its proposal that a clan should hold the presidency of the country. It is against this background that UNOSOM embarked upon finding a way to reconcile the leadership within the Hawiye clans. All their effort was concentrated on this end,

---

41. Run Doon, Somali Affairs, *Journal of the Anglo-Somali Society*, Spring Issue 1994, pp.5-7.
42. Mahamed Abshir "Waldo", "Somalia: The Need for a New Approach" from a Somali Point of View, Nairobi February 25, 1995.

and therefore they neglected other possible solutions. In fact, UNOSOM officials believed that the impasse in Somalia was fundamentally a question of who was to be the leader of the Hawiye clans. How could UNOSOM sustain the belief that the policy could be viable? A similar idea was responsible for the instability and resurgence of clan warfare after the warlords had failed to agree on a national political framework; clan rivalry over which clan would get the upper hand and the leading role had been at the root of the failure.

The roots of the civil war were considered to be the politicisation of the clans by the defunct military regime. But the clans had always been politicised. In the traditional Somali view of, and the overriding objection to Barre's regime was that it was based on clan domination. And until state institutions establish root in Somali society, it will be essential that clan equilibrium be maintained and political forces carefully balanced to share power.

CONCLUSION

The Breakdown of the State

After over a century of colonial defamation of Somali culture and two decades of repressive, centralised state control, involving the manipulation of clan mentality, the exploitation of traditional rivalry and the suppression and collective punishment for any form of rebellion, a destructive instinct was created in society which was at odds with the notion of Somali nationhood. The decrease in the political resources of the state, both institutional and human, and the failure to deliver the missing territories, undermined the state's effectiveness. And while the state's authority was waning, other, sub-national, forces of society were growing stronger, and soon the state was unable to withstand the tide which swept it aside.

In this anarchical situation traditional clan hostility, which during the colonial struggle had been extinguished, was reignited. There was a "reaffirmation of lineage identity and territoriality over national concern, a re-drawing of alliance, and struggle over the control of resources."[43] It marked an unprecedented turning point for the Somali state, with people returning to their clan "areas". The dispute in the north, between the Isaaq and the Ogaadeen in the last days of Siyaad Barre, the feud between the Majeerteen and the Habar Gidir (Hawiye) in the Mudug region in central Somalia, the confrontation between the Hawiye's Abgaal and Habar Gidir clans in Muqdisho, and the strife in Kismaayo between the Daarood's Harti and the Mahamed Subeer Ogaadeen, was over ownership and access to territory.

Given the weakening of the foundations of national unity, it was inevitable that the relative strength of lineage and clan institutions should became the dominant social theme.[44] In the urban situation, the clan became a political instrument used by greedy and ambitious leaders. The clan's power, position and influence were exploited for the benefit of its leaders, at the expense of its members.

A destructive political culture had been introduced into the political thinking of the Somalis, and had transformed the positive cultural values of nationhood. After twenty-one years of dictatorial rule followed by a half decade of civil war, Somali society had lost unity. It had experienced the cumulative erosion and decline of moral, social and cultural

---

43. Mark Bradbury, "Extract of A Report to the Inter-NGO Committee for Somalia (U.K.) About Southern Somalia," August 1991.
44. Abdullahi A. Mohamoud, The Demise of Post-Colonial State 1992 p.13.

values which a society shares. This development of - if I can borrow Mazrui's remark - "microtribalization" was in contrast to the "macrotribalization" which was the earlier vision of pan-Somalism.

Not only had the Somali state failed to replace the clan in nurturing the security of the individual Somali, it had actually become a threat to his being. Was it not natural, then, for the Somali to go back to his/her tribal roots? The political exploitation of the recent past had created resentments which turned into a mood of destruction towards the state and its institutions.

In searching for explanations for the unbelievable destructiveness we test out all kinds of notions and ideas. Is it that the need to destroy stems from 'the unbearable feeling of powerlessness', and therefore 'the need to remove all objects with which the individual has to compete'?.[45] Is it that life has an inner dynamism which, if curbed, decomposes or changes from creative energies into energies directed towards destruction?. Was the breakdown of the state, therefore, an inevitable process, following the systematic repressions of the preceding two decades of a dictatorial military regime in Somalia?

On Matters of Leadership

The alien system introduced by the colonialists to manipulate the traditional Somali institutions to their advantage was to have untold consequences in later years. Traditional institutions were eroded, which in turn created the landscape for the emergence of the modern leadership of

---

45. Erich Fromm, *The Fear of Freedom*, 1980, pp.155-56.

the 1960s. The colonial influence on the traditional *Akhil* system, was perhaps the most insidious.

Traditionally, Somali political authority was spread through the community as a whole, as there was no centre for political control. Clan leaders dealt with people politically on a face-to-face basis, and were responsible for all affairs concerning the clan and its relations with other clans. They claimed no rights as rulers over their people. The clan-leader had little executive power. "He presided over the assembly of elders (*shir*), but did not himself make the decisions" (*Ugaaska wuu guddoonshaaye, ma gooyo*).[46] Somali egalitarianism is encapsulated in the right of every man to a say in communal affairs. After lengthy discussion and analysis of the matter concerned, a decision in the *shir* is decided by consensus.

During the late 1930s to 1960s lineage politics were manipulated to serve the political needs of the colonisers. A new form of hierarchy was introduced, and chiefs, called *akhils*, were appointed by the colonial administration to represent and speak for the clan lineages. They were paid a stipend by the colonial administration, and given other concessions. These spokesmen were generally, for obvious reasons of convenience and availability, drawn from the urban areas. Although they were in theory representative of clan local interests, they were not necessarily in touch with grass roots issues; they were 'townies', and more concerned with larger lineage, not to mention personal, interest. The fact that they were paid by the colonial master undermined the

---

46. Lidwien Kapteijns, Le Verdic de L'Arbre (Go'aankii Geedka): Le Xeer Issa", Ali Moussa Iye, *Hal-Abuur*, Vol.I, No.1, Summer 1993, pp.33-35.

traditional source of authority.[47] It weakened the integrity of the clan, and diminished the *akhil's* accountability to the clan. Moreover, groups whose *akhils* collaborated with the colonial government were favoured, in order to tempt other groups to acquiesce under the colonial authority.[48] Thus, the lineages were politicised by the colonisers for 'divide and rule' purposes, and the system was successful in corroding the local institution of *shir* (assembly) and traditional leadership. Traditional chiefs thus became marginalised. Such social changes, which saw the shifting of influence from traditional (rural) leaders to a new urban leadership, lay down the foundation for the political parties which were to spring up as part of the independence movement.

Here we see the beginnings of the influence of hitherto unfamiliar modern westernised politics - which was to have far reaching consequences on the later-to-be-constituted Somali state. This imposed and alien system eroded the power of grassroots communal associations.

The Siyaad Legacy

The centralisation of the system of government following independence brought a new type of leadership. The ability of the traditional assemblies to influence decisions grew steadily weaker and power shifted to leaders who were elected to parliament. These new leaders, living away from the communities who had elected them, were free of the

---

47. Ahmed I. Samatar, *Socialist Somalia: Rhetoric and Reality*, 1988, p.49.
48. Sadia M Ahmed, Transformation of Somali Marriage System and Gender Relations, Unpublished MSc Dissertation, pp.28-30.

traditional pattern of constraints, and became less and less accountable for their actions.

This new political culture created a type of leader who was more concerned with personal power and aggrandisement. Such a person, physically and socially removed from the traditional power base, felt free to operate unchecked by the clan, and this lack of responsibility to his constituents was not compensated for by a more general, though essential, sense of responsibility to society that should accompany public service. This degeneration in standards of responsibility would help pave the way for the subsequent leadership crises during the military era, and in the period of disintegration of the Somali nation state.

After the power vacuum created by the downfall of Barre, the leadership of so called "warlords" which emerged, changed the course of events into widespread factional warfare of a primitive feudal nature. The "warlords" became indistinguishable from Siyaad Barre in deliberately destroying what remained of Somalia to satisfy their sadism and lust for power. In the opinion of Siciid F Maxamuud:

> Political organisations exercising the same programme [i.e. a clan-based programme (ed.)] as that of their opponent in government, could not be expected to bring about change.... The misreading of the warning signs by the opposition fronts precipitated the unsavoury consequence of today. A deadly trap of clan chauvinism for supremacy devoured the country at the very time when it deserved a worthwhile rest [from] years of civil war, economic deprivation and repression. It was a trap well set by the government, who then mastered

the intricacies of the game of 'clannism' - exploitation of the clan system for political ends - to consolidate their power. The explanation of the frenetic events after the downfall of President Siyaad Barre partly lies in the above — other than being an unfortunate episode of the weaknesses of clan superstructure, it is a triumphal manifestation of Siyaadist culture over the Somali identity and tradition.[49]

In spite of the fact that Siyaad Barre left the country after his downfall, his political culture, Siyaadism, which is "a system of destructive psychosis that overrides the cultural, traditional and spiritual values of Somali people"[50] prevailed in the country.

In the wake of the collapse of dictatorial rule, there were no national institutions or united opposition left to replace it. The consequent anarchy was due to the dictator having held all power in his hands, but also to the failure of the opposition movements to put aside personal ambitions and agree a common national framework.

This failure on the part of the opposition, highlights the poor quality of its political leadership. In the view of Mirreh:

> depending on the quality of its leaders [...] one country quickly embarks upon a dynamic course of development while another country steadily slips into the abyss of instability and disintegration let alone

---

49. Quoted in Siciid F Maxamuud, *Prisoners of Siyadist Culture*, *Hal-Abuur*.
50. Ibid, pp.16-17.

to attain a minimum tempo of economic and social progress.[51]

Somali leadership failed to set the country upon a dynamic course of national unity, stability and development. The leaders lacked vision, commitment, and moral fibre. Instead they were interested in satisfying their egos, and lust for power became contagious. The example of history forcefully suggests that such lust, unchecked, could easily spread to epidemic proportions,[52] and that is exactly what happened in Somalia, where the megalomania of a handful of individuals plunged the country into devastation and chaos. It was a chaos which had been nurtured by Barre's tribalization of Somali politics. Where maximum suspicion and mistrust among Somali clans had been created by the military regime. Where no clan could trust another.

The Rise of the Clan Militia

In the wake of the breakdown of law and order, the power- thirsty warlords or warleaders aggravated an already tense situation. It was necessary for each group or clan to rely on itself for its safety and defence, and to form its own militia. The clan militias were composed of young men, and organised by the clan elders. The fighters were maintained by their communities in return for their defence of the clan

---

51. Quoted in Hassan Ali Mirreh, "Providing for the Future", *The Somali Challenge,* Geneva 10-14 July 1992, p.17.
52. Swami Kriyanda, *Crisis in Modern Thought,* 1972, Vol.I p.10.

interests and for fighting off attacks from opposing clans.[53] In addition to the core groups of fighters there were the "freelance" militiamen called ***mooryaan, jirri*** or ***dayday*** who joined the factions or clans whenever their services were required.[54] Organised and encouraged by their leaders, this last group looted what the group required.[55] Much of the warlords's power was founded on a promise of protection, supremacy and spoils for their clans, and on the domination of others.[56] A State of Normality or of Anomaly?

During the decades when the disintegration of Somali institutions was taking place, modern institutions were not developing from within, or else did not have the underpinnings to endure. The ever-increasing economic and political chaos weakened and confused moral standards, and urban society became more and more tolerant of corruption (*musuqmaasuq*), the stealing of state property, black marketeering (*suuq madow*), etc. The concepts of theft, bribery and corruption became synonymous with the success of the individual.

Engulfed in such deep social crisis and the suspension of normality, the individual is faced with mental and moral confusion.

The moral frame of reference which the individual had previously relied on produced a discord when applied to the current state of affairs. In such a situation, and not knowing

---

53. Margaret A. Vogt, Demobilisation in Somalia, *Life & Peace Review*, Vol. 8, No.4, 1994, pp.26-29.
54. Ibid., pp.26-29.
55. Ibid., pp.26-29.
56. Human Rights Watch/Africa, Somalia Faces the Future: Human Rights in a Fragmented Society, Vol.7, No.2, April 1995, p.6.

which values to uphold, the individual may rid himself of the dissonance by changing his attitudes.

Such circumstances can be defined as an anomic state. Anomy is defined as "a state of normlessness which leaves man without moral guidance."[57] Emile Durkheim explains anomy as a "situation where the individual find himself in a state of mental and moral confusion. Such situations can be produced by several causes, such as contradictory economic forces, political chaos, certain ideological cleavage, and weak and confused moral standards."[58] He writes:

> [...] Irrespective of any external regulatory form, our capacity for feeling is in it itself an insatiable and bottomless abyss... But if nothing external can restrain this capacity, it can only be a source of torment to itself. Unlimited desires are insatiable by definition and insatiability is rightly considered a sign of morality. [...] when society is disturbed by some painful crisis or by beneficent but abrupt translation, it is momentarily incapable of exercising this [necessary and restraining] influence [on man's unlimited desires].[59]

This new moral code tolerated any action emanating from the use of crude power and violence. In this scenario, moral restraint was seen as the very height of human weakness.[60]

---

57. Ibid., pp.190-220.
58. Ibid., pp.204-210.
59. L.A. Coser and B. Rosenberg, eds. *Sociological Theory*, 1969, pp. 523-529.
60. Hassan Ali Mirreh, "Providing for the Future: Memory, Mutuality and Obligation", *The Somali Challenge: Peace, Resources*

CONCLUSION

The UN's Attempt to Again Shape Somalia

Under the auspices of the United Nations, a national reconciliation conference between the Somali warlords was held in Addis Ababa in mid-March 1993 and another one was held in Nairobi in March 1994. Though the Somalis and the world community were hopeful of seeing an end to the disastrous civil war, soon many were sceptical about getting a workable result from the conferences. The scepticism was based on the belief that these meetings, like that held in Djibouti in July 1991, had failed to address the real concerns.

Both meetings were dominated by the same warlords who were responsible for the civil strife, and the death and starvation of thousands of Somalis. The UN dealt with the warlords as if they were national leaders, without questioning their authority and legitimacy. Inevitably, the conferences gave the warlords international legitimacy and validated them as holding the keys to peace. And since UNOSOM's overall purpose was political reconstruction, political support at the highest level of UNOSOM's operations was reserved for initiatives involving the warlords.[61] The UN had by its own efforts boxed itself in.

Although peace talks in themselves could be considered a welcome breakthrough, the Nairobi peace accord was a complete turnabout from the previous peace process which was concluded in Addis Ababa exactly one year before. The latter had adopted a grass-roots approach — first to

---

and Reconstruction, Geneva 10-14 July 1992, p.16-7.
61. Human Rights Watch/Africa, Somalia Faces the Future, Vol.7, No.2, April 1995, pp. 4-5.

create district councils before setting up the top levels of administration.

With these actions, the UN failed to endeavour honestly to tackle the issue of peace. Instead, it set about undermining already attained peace areas. In the North-Eastern Region and the self-proclaimed Somaliland Republic, the UN denied the help required to maintain the fragile peace that had been painfully fashioned.[62] The gravest condemnation of UNOSOM in the Somali context is that it failed to consider seriously any Somali initiative.

After nearly five decades, the UN was again involved in shaping the future of Somalia but without learning from its previous mistakes. The colonial denial, with the UN's blessing, of Somali aspirations had greatly affected the psyche of the Somali nation. And again, UNOSOM II, wearing the UN mantle frustrated any genuine peace initiatives, so demonstrating their lack of understanding of the real local situation.

The UN's latest impotency in Somali was, sadly, soon to be repeated in other world trouble spots, where genocide was again unleashed against whole populations and the UN was found wanting.

The State and the OAU

In the wake of the decolonisation of Africa, it was anticipated that the inherited colonial boundaries would generate bitter conflicts among the newly emerging countries

---

62. See Ahmed Yusuf Farah with Professor I M Lewis, *Somalia: Roots of Reconciliation*. See also "Shirka Nabadda iyo Nolosha ee Garoowe" Diseembar 16-28 1993, Garoowe, Northeastern Region.

of the continent. The borders which many of the states inherited were patently unrealistic and unjust. But for some states, a realigning of borders would pose a threat to their existence. To tackle these and other problems, to be a voice for Africa in the arena of world politics, and in the spirit of pan-Africanism, African leaders established the Organisation of African Unity (OAU), in 1963.

The colonial disputes and interests in the nineteenth century resulted in the partition of the Somali territory into five parts. As a result, on independence in July 1960, a large number of the Somali people remained outside the boundaries handed over to Somalia by the colonial powers. Moreover, the colonial powers left behind a centralised system of government alien to the Somalis.

Nonetheless, for the Somali people the creation of an independent Somali Republic on 1 July, 1960 was only the beginning of their struggle for national unity, and although it linked those Somalis formerly ruled by Italian and British colonial powers, it excluded those living in Ethiopia, Kenya, and Djibouti.

Unfortunately, the OAU failed to solve the basic conflicts over national borders, and rather complicated the whole issue by accepting the *status quo* on colonial-drawn boundaries in Africa.

The Somali Republic's policy of uniting her remaining kinsmen under one flag effectively isolated it from the pan-African movement. However, Somalis themselves did not see that having pan-Somalism as the driving force of their foreign policy contradicted their pan-Africanism. They regarded it as an application of the wider principle, since it aimed at a legitimate unification of territories which colonialists's interests had arbitrarily destroyed. Many OAU member-states, however, saw Somalia's position on borders as troublesome and potentially divisive, and were not well-disposed towards her.

The State's Painful Demise

In December 1990 the Somali state collapsed into disarray, and since January 1991 has lacked any kind of central government authority.

Some of the things which impacted on the eventual collapse are discussed in the preceding chapters. Among these are: the undermining of traditional authority over decades; the shortcomings of alien notions of government - the parliamentary system during the independence decade which failed to meet the high hopes of the people and failed to deliver the missing territories, the two decades of Scientific Socialism which spawned Siyaadism and which completely destroyed the moral fabric of the society; neo-colonial super-power interests in the Horn which left it littered with weaponry; boundary problems with neighbours which would not go away and which were ignored by the OAU; in the absence of a benevolent state, the reversion of the people to old clan loyalties, and with it the loss of a pan-Somali vision.

The conditions and attitudes which may help bring eventual peace to the Somalis are not part of this discussion, though some may have been hinted at. At the time of writing, almost six years of unrelenting clan fighting has continued. In January 1995, Siyaad Barre, the dictator of twenty-one years, whose overthrow sent Somalia spinning out of control, died in exile in Nigeria. As this book was going to press General Mahamed Farah Aydiid, most prominent and notorious of the warlords of the civil war period, died in Muqdisho of wounds suffered as a result of violent conflict. Again Somaliland will be reconstituted, but when and in what form cannot yet be predicted.

APPENDIX

Appendix I

Agreement signed by Ahmed Murgan, Chief of the Ogaden Tribe, placing his country under British Protection. 1st September, 1896.[63]

    I, Ahmed Murgan, the Chief of the Ogaden tribe, do hereby place myself, my people, and country, with its dependencies, under the protection of Her Britannic Majesty the Queen, and do hereby declare that I will not, nor shall my successors or any of my people, cede or alienate any portion of my territories or independencies, or make any Treaties with any foreign State or person, without the previous knowledge and sanction of Her Majesty's Government.

    Commercial arrangements between me and non-natives shall be subject to the approval of Her Majesty's

---

63. Hertslet, E. The Map of Africa by Treaty, p.387.

Representative, who shall regulate all disputes, and by whose I will be guided in all my relations with non-natives.
Witness:
(Signatures in Arabic)
Before me,
J.W. Tritton

A.C.W. Jenner,
Sub-Commissioner.

Appendix II

Treaty of Friendship and Protection between France and the Chiefs of the Issa Somalis. Obock, 26th March, 1885.[64]

Between M. Lagarde (A.M.J.L), Governor of the Colony of Obock, acting in the name of the French Government, and the Issa Chiefs hereinafter defined:-

Abdi Handel, Roble Tonke, Barre Ali, Beder Gedi, Gedi Dagah, Dirane Dedis, Roble Guled, Hassan Gedi, Gedi Roble, Muse Said, Maherame Ige, Waes Garbabud, Gedi Hersi, Geri Jibelbor, Allale Waes, Assobi Bonis, Oure Barre, Waes Guled, Buhe Dirir, who control the territory extending from Gubbet Kharak and beyond Ambaddo near Zeyla, the following Treaty has been signed:-

Art. I - There shall henceforth be eternal friendship between France and the Chiefs of Issa.

Art. II- The Chiefs of the Issa hand over their territory to France that she may protect it against all foreign.

---

64. Ibids., p.633.

Art. III- The France Government undertakes to facilitate commerce on the coast and especially at Ambaddo.

Art. IV - The Issa Chiefs undertake to assist France at all times and to sign no Treaty nor conclude any agreement, under penalty of nullity, without the consent of the Governor of Obock.

Done at Obock, the 26th March, 1885.

(sd) Lagarde,
Governor of the Colony

(Mark of the Issa Chiefs)

Appendix III

Agreement of Peace and Protection between the Italian Government and Sheikh Mohammed-ben-Abdullah (Mullah). Signed at Illig, 5th March, 1905.[65]

(Translation from the Arabic.)

Praise to the Merciful God!

In accordance with the common desire of the Contracting Parties to afford peace and tranquillity to all Somalis, Cavaliere Pestalozza, the special Envoy acting under the authority of the Italian Government, and Said Mohammed-ben-Abdullah, acting for himself and for the Chief and Notables of the tribes following him, have agreed on the compete acceptance of the following clauses and conditions:

---

65. Ibids., p.1120.

1. There shall be peace and lasting accord between the above-mentioned Said Mohammed-ben-Abdullah, with his above-mentioned Dervishes, and the British Government, with all its dependents among the Somali and other. So, likewise, shall there be peace between the Said, with his above mentioned Dervishes, and the Government of Abyssinia, with all its dependents. The Italian Government guarantee and pledge themselves on behalf of their dependents, as also on behalf of the British Government.

Every disagreement or difference between the Said and his people and the dependents of the Italian Government, or those for whom the Government have pledged themselves — as, for example, the English and their dependents — shall be settled in a peaceful and friendly manner by means of "erko" or of Envoy from the two parties under the presidency of an Italian Delegate, and also in the present of an English Envoy whenever British interests are concerned.

2. Said Mohammed-ben-Abdullah is authorized by the Italian Government to establish for himself and his people a fixed residence at the point most convenient for communication with the sea, between Ras Garad and Ras Gabbe.

This also with the approval of Yusuf Ali (Sultan of Obbia) and Sultan Osman Mahmud (Sultan of Migertini).

That residence and all its inhabitants shall be under the protection of the Italian Government and under their flag.

If and when the Italian Government so desire, they shall be at liberty to instal in that residence a Representative of Italian nationality, or other person, as Governor, with soldier and custom-house (or tithes).

Said Mohammed shall in every way afford help and support to the Government in all matters, and until the Government appoint a special Representative of their own the said Said Mohammed shall be their Procurator.

The government of the tribes subject to him in the interior shall remain in the hands, of Said Mohammed, and shall be exercised with justice and equity.

Moreover, he shall provide for the security of the roads and the safety of the caravans.

3. In the above-mentioned residence, commerce shall be free for all, subject to the Regulations and Ordinance of the Government. However, from henceforth the importation and disembarkation of fire-arms, cartridges, lead and powder necessary for the same, is prohibited. Said Mohammed himself and his people pledge themselves by a formal and complete pledge, as also by oath before God, to prevent the traffic, importation, and disembarkation of slaves and fire-arms whencesoever they may come, whether by sea or land.

Whoever shall infringe this Ordinance shall be liable to such punishment as shall be considered fitting by the Government.

4. The territory assigned to Said Mohammed and his followers is that of the Nogal and the Hod comprised within the limits of the Italian sphere of interest (this territory lies between the Sultanates of Obbia and the Migirtini). But in view of the special Agreement between the Government of Italy and England, after the despatch and return of the "erko" (Somali delegation) sent to establish peace with the English according to Somali customs, and to settle

certain formalities necessary for the general tranquillity, the English shall authorize Said Mohammed and his followers to enter their territories (those of the English) in the country of the Nogal, to feed their cattle there according to their former custom.

But the said cattle shall not be permitted to pass beyond the pasturage of the wells enumerated hereafter; they are the wells of Halin, and from these to those of Hodin, and from Hodin to Tifafle, and from Tifafle to Danot.[66]

In the same manner, also, in the case of the Mijjerteins, there shall be accord and peace between them all and Said Mohammed and all his Dervishes.

The land of Mudug and Galcaio shall continue to belong to Yusuf Ali and his sons.

The question of the pasturage which is at issues these latter and the Issa Mahmud, as also between them and the Omar Mahmud, shall be settled with the approval and consent of the parties according to former custom.

All questions between the Dervishes and their neighbours shall be referred to the examination and the decision of the Italian Government.

In confirmation of all that is above stated, and as a pledge of the Contracting Parties, this document has been signed in duplicated by Said Mohammed-ben-Abdullah for himself and the Dervishes his followers, and by Cavaliere Pestalozza, the authorized Delegated of the Italian Government, at Illig,

---

66. This line was modified by Agreement between Great Britain and the Italian Government of 19th March, 1907, as follows: From Halin to Hodin, Hodin to Tifafle, Tifafle to Baran, Baran to Danot, Danot to Kurmis.

Sunday, the 28th if the month of Zelheggia, in the year 1322 of Hegira, corresponding to the 5th March in the year 1905.

I have read the above document and understood its entire contents, have accepted it all in perfect sincerity, and have signed it — in short, Cavaliere Pestalozza, Representative, knows my state — in good faith.

Sayed Mohammed-ben-Abdullah
Cavaliere Pestalozza

Illig, 5th March, 1905.

MAPS: Abyssinian Expansion from 1887-1891

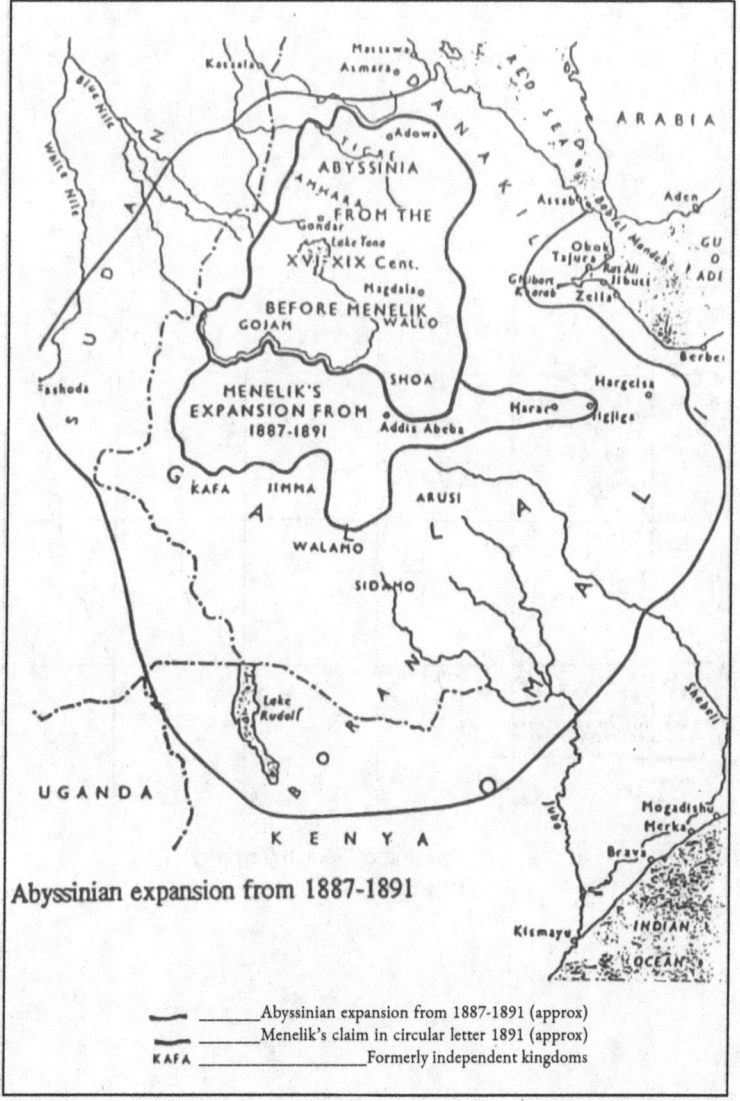

Partition of Somali Territory between 1888-1894

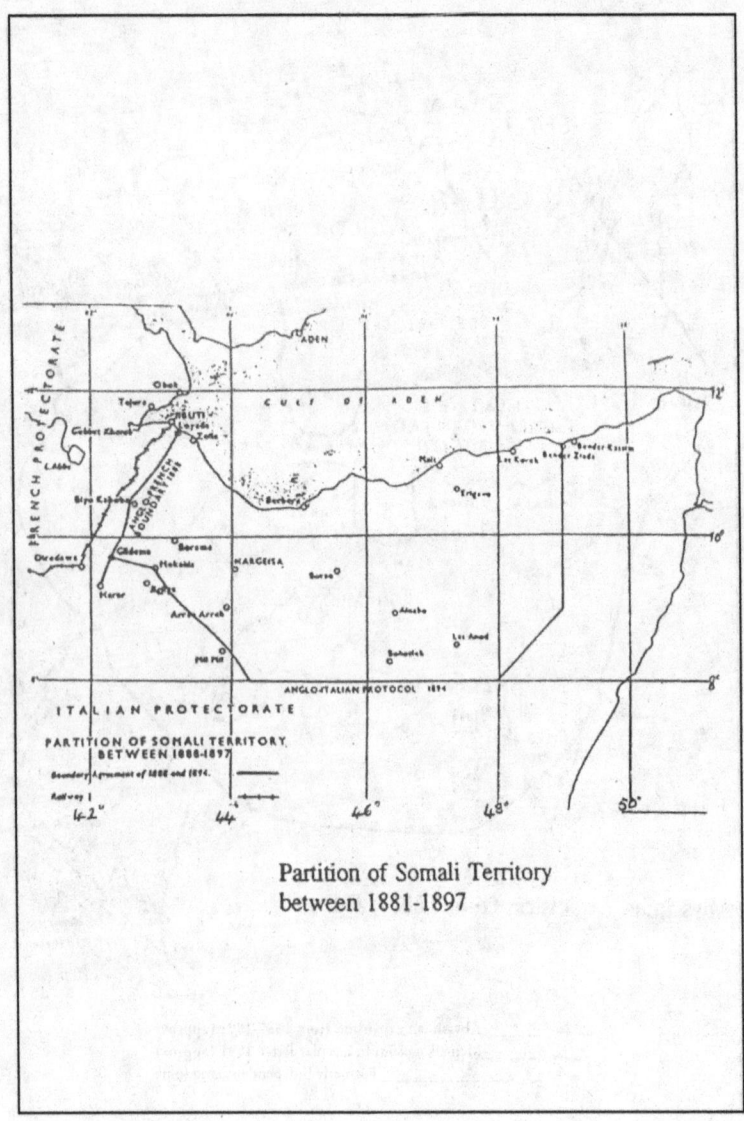

Partition of Somali Territory between 1881-1897

Partition of East Africa into Spheres of Influence 1890-91

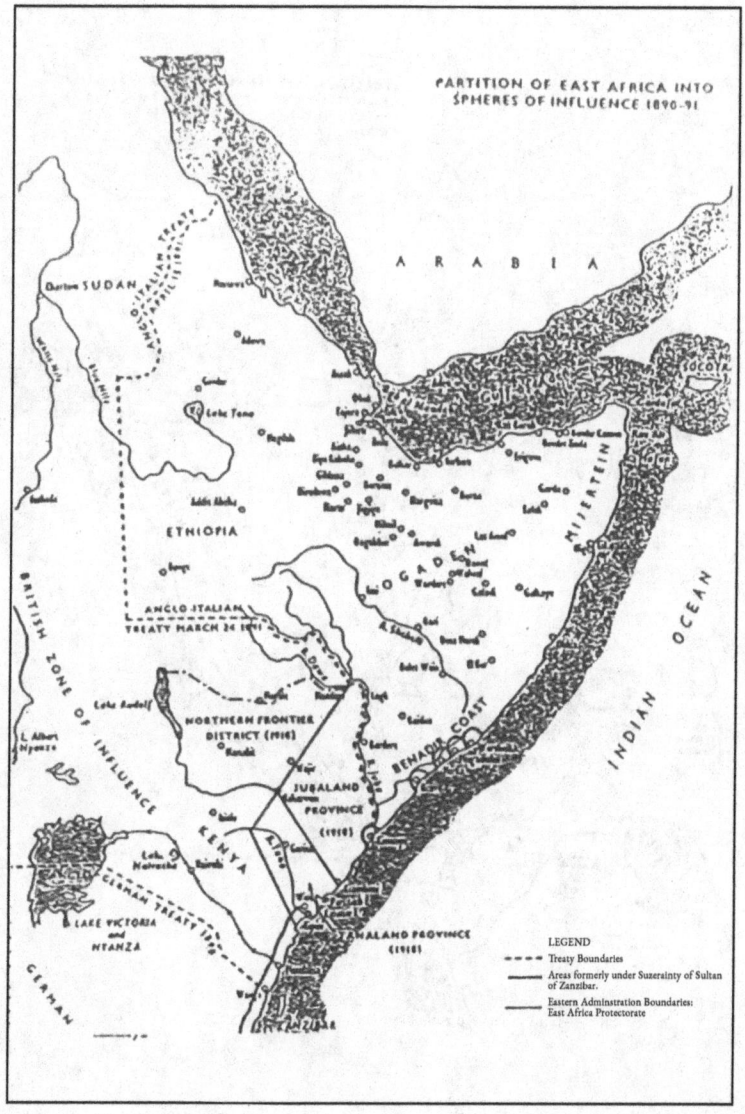

Secession of Jubbaland

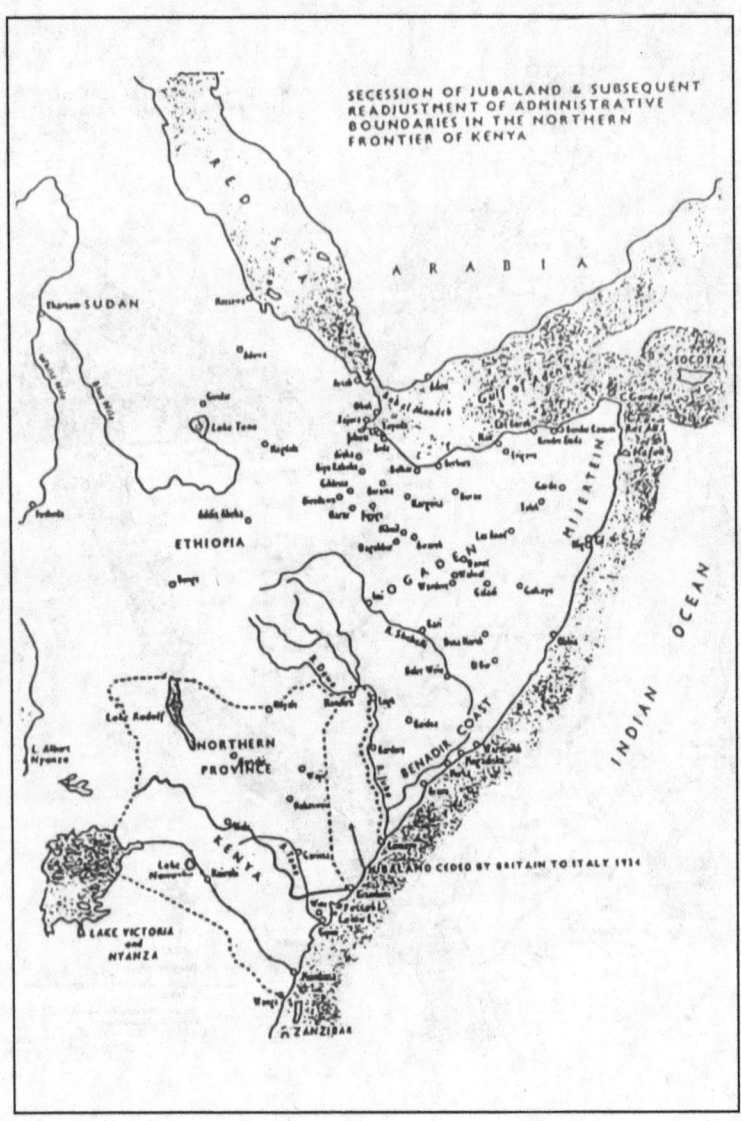

North-Eastern Sultanates

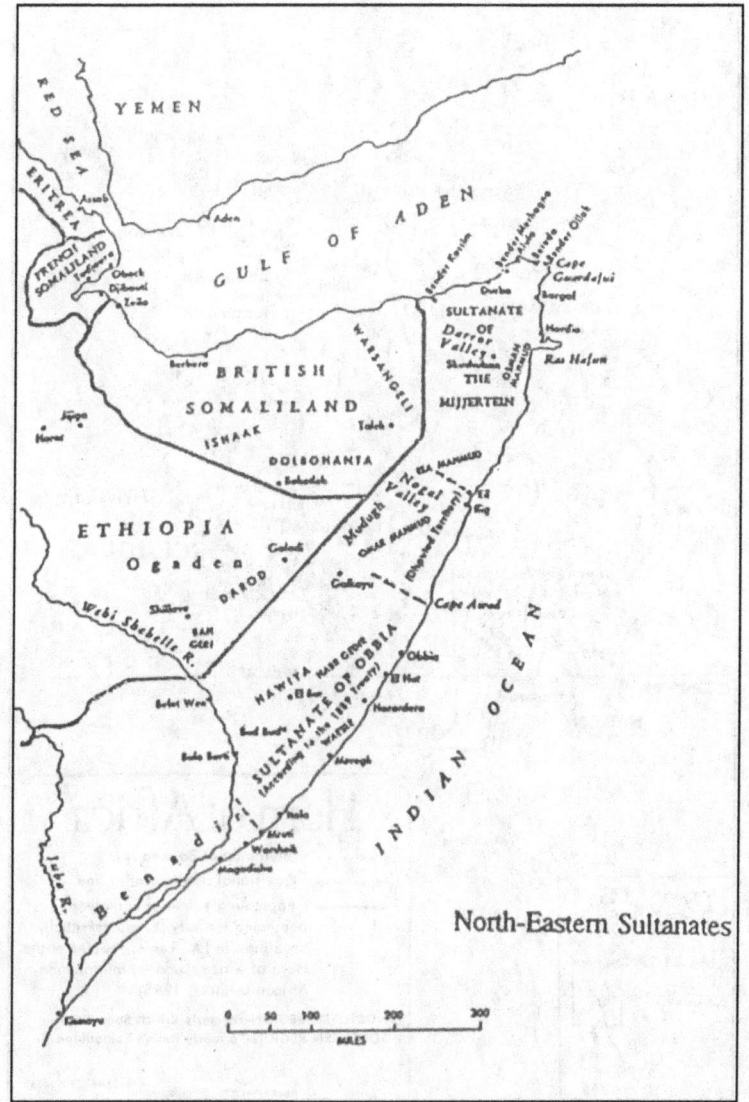

Somali-Populated Territory

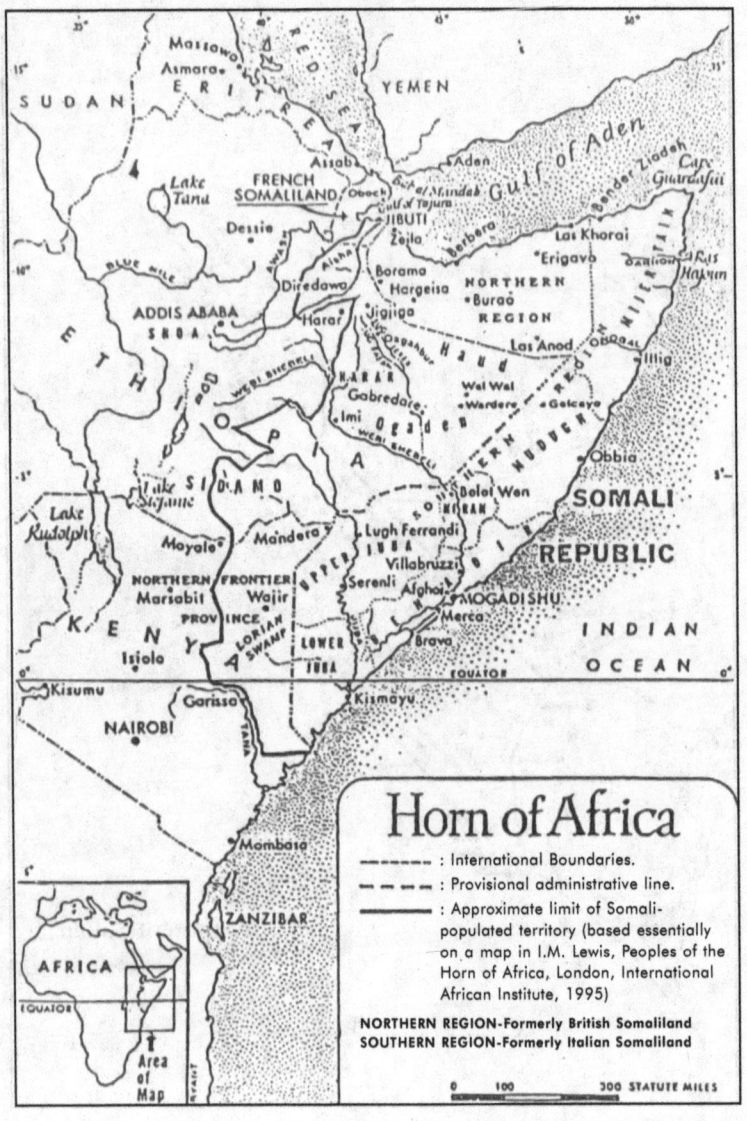

Somalia

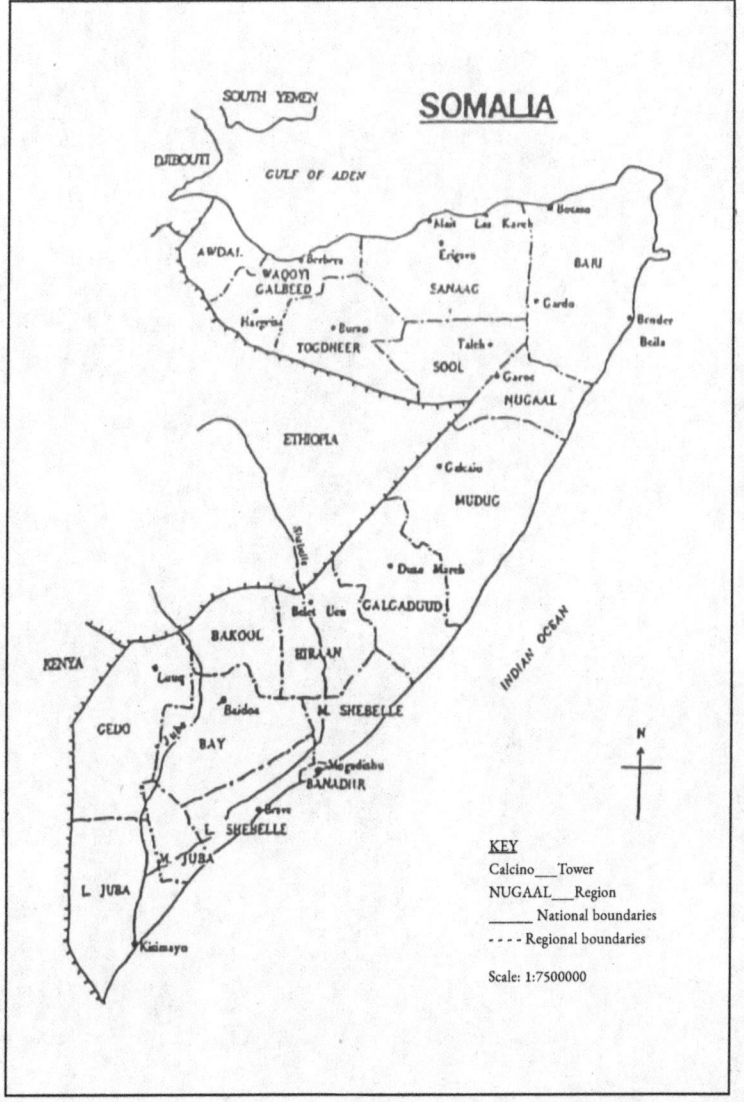

BIBLIOGRAPHY

Selected Works

Afrah, Maxamed D.; "The Mirror of Culture: Somali Dissolution Seen Through Oral Expression" in *The Somali Challenge: From Catastrophe to Renewal?* ed. by Ahmed I. Samatar, (Boulder, Colorado: Lynne Rienner Publishers, 1994).

Andrezejewski B. W., and Lewis, I. M., *Somali Poetry: An Introduction*, (Oxford: University of Oxford, 1964).

Aw Jaamac Cumar Ciise, *Taariikhdii Daraawiishta iyo Sayid Maxamed Cabdulle Xasan, (1895-1921)*, Wasaaradda Hiddaha iyo Tacliinta Sare, Akadeemiyaha Dhaqanka, Muqdishu, 1976.

Burton, Isabel; ed., First Footsteps in East Africa by Captain Sir Richard F. Burton, Vol.I, (London: Tylston and Edwards, 1894).

Cabdulqaadir Shire Faarah, *Xeebtii Geerida*, London, July 1990.

Caroselli, Francesco; *Ferro e Fuoco in Somalia*, (Roma: Sindicato Italiano Arti Grafiche Editore, 1931).

Coser, L.A. and Rosenberg, B.; eds., *Sociological Theory,* (New York: Macmillan 1969 edn.).
De Vecchi di Val Cismon, Cesare Maria; *Orizzonti d'Impero: Cinque Anni in Somalia,* (Milano: A. Mondatori, 1935)
Farah, Mohammed I.; *From Ethnic Response to Clan Identity: A Study of State Penetration among the Somali Nomadic Pastoral Society of Northeastern Kenya,* (Doctoral Dissertation at Uppsala University, Uppsala 1993).
Fitzgibbon, Louis; *The Betrayal of the Somalis,* (London: Rex Collings Ltd., 1982)
Government of the Somali Republic, *The Somali Peninsula: A New Light on Imperial Motives,* Information Services of the Government of Somali, Mogadishu, 1962.
Gergen, Kenneth J.; Gergen, and Mary J.; *Social Psychology,* (New York: Harcourt Brace Jovanovich, Inc, 1981) p.34.
Giner, Salvator; *Sociology,* (London: Martin Robertson, 1975).
Gobban, Alfred; *National Self-determination,* (London Oxford University Press 1945).
Drake-Brockman and Ralph E., *British Somaliland,* (Hurst and Blackett, London, 1912).
Hersi, Abdirahman Ali; *The Arab Factor in Somali History: The Origins and the Development of Arab Enterprise and Cultural Influences in the Somali Peninsula,* (Ph.D. dissertation, University of California, Los Angels, 1977).
Hess, Robert L.; *Italian Colonialism in Somalia,* (Chicago: The University of Chicago Press, 1966).
Hertslet, E. *The Map of Africa by Treaty,* (London).
ILO, *Generating Employment and Income in Somalia,* Report of an ILO/JASPA Inter-Disciplinary Employment and Project-Identification Mission to Somalia, ILO, United Nations Development Programme, Addis Ababa, 1989.
Jardine, Douglas; *The Mad Mullah of Somaliland,* (London: Herbert Jarkins, 1932).

Jones, A H M; and Monroe, Elizabeth; *A History of Abyssinia*,(Oxford: Oxford University Press, 1937).

Kaplan, Irvin; ....[and others], *Area Handbook for Somalia: Political*, (Washington DC: American University, 1969).

King, Preston; *An African Winter; Somalia: State of War*, (Harmondsworth: Penguin, 1986).

Kriyanda, Swami; *Crisis in Modern Thought*, Vol.I, (Nevada City, California: Ananda Publications, 1972).

Lee, Cassenelli; *The Shaping of Somali Society*, (Philadelphia: University of Pennsylvania Press, 1982).

Lewin, Moshe; *The Gorbachev Phenomenon: A Historical Interpretation*, (London: Hutchinson Radius, 1988).

Lewis I. M.; *A Pastoral Democracy*, (London: Oxford University Press, 1961).

------ *Peoples of the Horn of Africa: Somali, Afar and Saho*, 2nd edn. (London: Haan Associates for the International African Institute), 1994.

------ *A Modern History of Somalia: Nation and State in the Horn of Africa* (London: Longman, 1980).

------ *Understanding Somalia: A Guide to Somali Culture, History and Social Institutions*, (London: Haan Associates, 1993).

Luling, Virginia; *The Social Structure of Southern Somali Tribes*, (Doctoral thesis, University of London, 1971).

Makakis, John; "The Isaq-Ogaden Dispute," in *Ecology and Politics: Environment Stress and Security in Africa*, ed. by Anders Hjort af Ornäs et al. (Scandinavian Institute of African Studies, 1989).

Martin, Bradford G.; *Muslim Politics and Resistance to Colonial Rule: Shaykh Uways Bin Muhammed Al-Baraawi and the Qadiriya Brotherhood in East Africa*, Journal of African History, 10,3 (1969).

Mazrui, Ali; and Tidy, Michael; *Nationalism and New States of Africa*, (Nairobi: Heinemann, 1984).

Miller, David; ed., *Blackwell Encyclopedia of Political Thought*, (Oxford: Basil Blackwell Ltd., 1987).

Moyse-Barlett, H.; *The History of the King's African Rifles*, 1956.

Perham, Margery; *The Government of Ethiopia*, (Evanston, Illionios: North Western University Press, 1969).

Omar, Mohamed Osman; *The Road to Zero: Somalia's Self-Destruction*, (London: Haan Associates, 1992).

Raikes, Philip; "Food Shortages and Famine," in *Society & Social Science: A Reader*, ed. by James Anderson et al., (The Milton Keynes: Open University Press, 1990).

Oliver, Roland; and Crowder, Michael; eds., *The Cambridge Encyclopedia*, (Cambridge: Cambridge University Press, 1981).

Sagan, Eli; *At the Dawn of Tyranny: The Origins of Individualism, Political Oppression, and the State*, (London: Faber and Faber, 1985).

Samatar, Ahmed I.; *Socialist Somalia: Rhetoric and Reality*, (London Zed Books Ltd, 1988).

------ "The Curse of Allah: Civic Disembowelment and the Collapse of the State in Somalia", in *The Somali Challenge: From Catastrophe to Renewal?* ed. by Ahmed I. Samatar, (Boulder, Colorado: Lynne Rienner Publishers, 1994).

Samatar, Said S.; *Oral Poetry and Somali Nationalism: The Case of Sayid Mahammad 'Abdille*, (Cambridge: Cambridge University Press, 1982).

------ *Somalia: A Nation In Turmoil*, A Minority Rights Group, August 1991.

Samatar, Said S.; and Laitan, David D.; *Somalia: Nation in Search of a State*, (Bouler, Colorado: Westview Press, 1987).

Sheikh-Abdi, Abdi; *Divine Madness: Mohammed Abdulle Hassan (1856-1920)* (London: Zed Books Ltd., 1992).

Touval, Saadia; *Somali Nationalism: International Politics and the Drive for Unity in the Horn of Africa*, (Cambridge: Harvard University Press, 1963).

Trimingham, Spencer J.; *Islam in Ethiopia*, (Oxford: the Clarendon Press, 1952).

Zillmann, Dolf; *Hostility and Aggression*, (Hillsdale, New Jersey: Lawrence Erlbaum Associates Publishers, 1979).

Papers and Reports

Abdisalam Issa-Salwe/Cabdisalaam M Ciise-Salwe, "The Collapse of Somali National State: The Colonial Factor," in *Paix et Reconstruction en Somalie*," Paris, 15-17 April 1993.

African Events, "Mogadishu Burning", February 1991.

------ "In Search of Stability", *African Events*, April 1991. Amnesty International, "Somalia: A Human Rights Disaster," Al-Index:AFR-52/01/92, 1992.

------ *Somalia: A Government at War with its Own People*, (New York: Human Rights Watch, 1990).

------ "Somalia: Update on a Disaster - Proposals for Human Rights," AI Index: Afr 52/01/93, 30 April 1993.

------ "Somalia", AI Index: Afr 52/11/85, July 1985.

Bradbury, Mark; and Davies, Rick; "A Report of the Assessment Mission to Bari, Nugaal, and Mudug Regions of Somalia from September 17th to September 30th to the Inter-NGO Committee for Somalia (UK)," October 1991.

Cassanelli V Lee; and Banafunzi, Bana M S; "A Recent Poetic Lament from Brava", 199?.

Farah, Ahmed Yusuf; with Professor I M Lewis; "Somalia: Roots of Reconciliation"

Hassan Osman Ahmed, "La Cittá di Marka, I Biimaal e il Dominio sulla Costa Somala: La Prima Colonizzazione Italiana del Benadir, ca.1800 - 1910", PhD dissertation, (Universitá degli

Studi di Napoli, Istituto Universitario Orientale, Facoltá di Scienza Politiche, 1994).

Human Rights Watch/Africa, "Somalia Beyond the Warlords: The Needs for a Verdict on Human Rights Abuses," Vol.V, Issue No.2, 7 March 1993.

------ "Somalia Faces the Future: Human Rights in a Fragmented Society", Vol.7, No.2, April 1995.

Human Rights Watch/Africa & Physicians For Human Rights, "Somalia: No Mercy in Mogadishu", March 26, 1992.

Lewis, I.M.; "The Death and Birth of the Somali State."

Menkhaus, Ken; "Statement Regarding the Status of the Barawan (Bravan) People of Coastal Southern Somalia", May 3, 1993.

Mirreh, Hassan Ali; "Providing for the Future: Memory, Mutuality and Obligation," in *The Somali Challenge: Peace, Resources and Reconstruction*, Geneva, 10-14 July 1992.

Mohamed Abshir "Waldo", "Somalia: The Need for a New Approach from a Somali Point of View", Nairobi February 25, 1995.

Mohamed, Mohamed-Abdi; "Autopsie de la crise: les enjeux nationaux, regionuax et internationaux*"; Forum: La guerre civile en Somalie: Quand? Comment? Pourquoi?*, Paris, 7 et 8 Avril 1992.

Mohamoud, Abdullahi A.; "The Demise of Post-Colonial State: A Case Study of Contemporary Conflict in Somalia," (The Institute of Social Study, the Hague 1992).

Rashid Mahamed "Gambon", "The Anatomy of The Civil War: Somalia in Post-Independence" in *Conference on Current Events in Somalia,* Nairobi, 18 October 1993.

Sadia Muse Ahmed "Transformation of Somali Marriage System and Gender Relations: Rhetoric and Realities," Unpublished MSc dissertation, University of London, 1994.

"Shirka Nabadda iyo Nolosha ee Garoowe" Diseembar 16-28 1993, Garoowe, Northeastern Region.

Documents and Miscellaneous Papers

"Addis Ababa Agreement of the First Session of the Conference on National conciliation in Somalia," 27th March 1993.

Constitution of Somalia, Mogadiscio, July 1, 1962.

"Gaalkacyo Falls into the USC Hand, USC Military Communiqué," Ref. No. USC/DD/3/3/91, March 3, 1991.

"Maktabka Jihaadka," 25.10.14 (Hijra).

"The Jubbaland Peace Conference (Kismaayo)."

Waruhiu & Muite, "Mass Executions in Kismaayo, Somalia: A Case for Inquiry and Intervention," Nairobi, Kenya, January 8, 1993.

Yousuf Duhul, "A Letter to My Faqash Friend," 21 October 1988.

Periodicals and Newspapers

Bone, James; "UN Prepares to Assume Sole Charge of Governing Somalia", *Times*, 5th March 1993.

Daily Telegraph, "UN Told to Quit Somali Airport", November 14, 1992.

Economist, "Making Monkeys of the UN", July 10, 1993. Greenfield, Richard; "Somalia After the Fall", *Africa Report*, March-April 1991.

Himilo, "Dowlad Goboleed Lagu Dhawaaqay", Cadadka 22aad, Garoowe, 3 Janaayo 1992.

Horn of African Bulletin, "Mogadishu in Blood", January- February 1992.

------ "Operation Restore Hope?", Vol.4, No.6, Nov-Dec. 1992.

------ "A Clan Integrated Army", January-February 1992.

Huband, Mark; "Somalia Women Wage War in Town Split by Terrorism", *Monitor*, March 23, 1993.

------ "UN Troops Move into Mogadishu", *Guardian*, 14 September 1992.

------ "Relief Workers in Somalia Reject More UN Troops", *Guardian*, 10 September 1992.

------ "UN Troops Will Face Somali Bandit Threat to Food Aid", *Guardian*, 9 September 1992.
Guardian, "While the World Hesitate", 15th September 1992.
------ "The Starved of Hope", 15th September 1992.
------ "A Far Cry from The Weary Front", 15th September 1992.
Ilwaad Jaamac, "Who am I?", *Hal-abuur*, Vol.1, No.4, Spring 1995.
Kapteijns, Lidwien; "Le Verdict de L'Arbre (Go'aanka Geedka): Le Xeer Issa, Etude d'une Democratie Pastorale" by Ali Mouse Iye, *Hal-Abuur*, Vol.1, No.1, Summer 1993.
Kiley, Sam; "Somali Warlords Hoard Weapons as US Airlift Begins", *Times*, 29 August 1992.
Lewis, I M; "In the Land of the Living Dead", *Sunday Times*, 30 August 1992.
Maryan Cumar Cali and Lidwien Kapteijns, "A Cry for Independence: A Poem from Djibouti About the Agony of Colonial Oppression", *Hal-Abuur*, Vol.1, Nos.2&3, Autumn/Winter 1993/94.
Orwin, Martin; "Language and Poetry: An Inextricable Link", *Hal Abuur*, Vol.1, No.1, Summer 1993, pp.24-27.
Ozanne, Julian; "Somali Gunmen Hold Aid Agencies to Ransom as Thousands Starve to Death", *Financial Times*, 6 November 1992.
------ "UN's Plans Anger Somali Strongman", *Financial Times*, September 3, 1992.
Parmelee, Jennifer; "Famine and War" *International Herald Tribune*, 12th November 1992.
Perlez, Jane; "Somali Killed 100 as US Troops Landed", *International Herald Tribune*, Tuesday, December 29, 1992.
Peterson, Carl M.; and Barkely, Daniel T.; "Formula for Somalia", *New African*, June 1993.
Rakiya Omaar, "Somalia's Nightmare", *West Africa*, 17-23, 1993.

Siciid Faarah Maxamuud, "Prisoners of Siyadist Culture", *Hal-Abuur*, Vol.1, No.1, Summer 1993.
Walker, Martin; "30.000 US troops Get Aid Role", *Guardian*, 27th November 1992.
------ "UN Chief Urges Force to Help Somalia", *Guardian*, 1 December 1992.
Vogt, Margaret A., "Demobilisation in Somalia", *Life & Peace Review*, Vol. 8, Number 4, 1994.
West Africa, "Poor Man's War Unveiled", 17-23 August 1992.

INDEX

A.H. Hardinge 13
Abasguul 90
Abdi Hashi Dhorre 75
Abdiasis Nuur Hersi 71
Abdirahman Ahmed 109
Abdirahman Aw-Ali 110
Abdirahman Aw-Ali Farah 110
Abdirisaq Abubakar 92
Abdirisaq Haji Husein 65, 68, 106
Abdullahi Isse 49
Abdullahi Yusuf 84, 88, 110
Abdulqadir Dheel 74
Abgaal 74, 94, 96, 102, 103, 107, 121
Absame 90, 92, 93
Abyssinia xiii, 11, 14, 15, 20, 36, 38, 43, 62, 133
Adan Abdullahi 92, 113, 117
Adan Abdulle 49, 63-65, 68, 106
Aden 1, 11, 12, 22, 27, 34, 49, 59
Afar 1, 3, 53, 54, 56, 69

Afgooye 16, 18, 91, 104, 114
Agaar-weyne 26
Ahmed Dini 54
Ahmed Gurey 43
Ahmed Omar 93, 102, 113
Ahmed Saleebaan 71
Akhil 5, 51, 122
Ali Geri 26
Ali Hagarrey 94
Ali Mahdi 101, 103, 105, 107, 116, 117
Ali Sugulle 83
Ali Wardhigley 94
Alula 35, 36, 39, 86
Amhara Highlands 13
Anglo-German Agreement 12
Anglo-Italian Treaty 34
Antonio Cecchi 15, 17
Arab League 106
Arusha 57, 66
Arusi 33

Asharaaf 2
Aweera 1
Aydiid 71, 87, 94, 99, 103, 107, 110, 116, 118, 119, 130
Ayl 27, 40
Ayr 96
Ba'aad-weyn 86
Baal-ad 90, 93
Baargaal 34, 39
Bajuun 2
Balan-balle 86
Balli-busle 86
Bandar Beyla 86
Bandhabow 2
Bar-da'ad 85
Barawe 2, 108
Bareeda 35
Bari 30, 75, 85, 86, 104, 105, 110
Bartire 90
Bayra 86
Beeldaaje 4
Beerdhiga 26
Benaadir 15, 19, 22, 28, 33, 35, 36, 41, 46, 102, 112
Bender Khassim 35
Berbera 11, 21-24, 28, 30, 76, 77, 109
Berlin 15
Bevin Plan 45, 52
Biyamaal 16-19, 28, 46
Boni 1
Boosaaso 35
Boqor 15, 26, 27, 34, 35, 39-41, 98, 110, 112
Boqor Osman 15, 27, 34, 35 39-41, 112

Bosaso 86
Britain 11-14, 23, 33, 43-45, 47, 48, 50-52, 56, 60, 66, 75, 76, 134
British Somaliland 49
Brussels General Act 13
Bud Bud 38
Bur-o' 50, 89, 90
Burtinle 86
busta rosso 65
Buuhodle 20, 24
Cairo 35, 54, 61
Camel Corps 30, 31
Carl von der Decken 11
Charles Guillain 11
Cold War 75, 76, 116, 119
Corpo Zaptié 36
Count Porro 11
Cuban 82
Cushitic 1, 54
Cyrenaica 44
Daar-ilaalo 30
Daarood 2, 51, 74, 90, 91, 93, 96, 98, 101-105, 107, 110-114
Daaroodiya 93
Dameero 30
Danakil 1
Daratoole 26
Dareema-addo 24
De Cuellar 117
De Vecchi 33, 36-41
Deelley 73
Derge 82
Dhabar Jebin 72
Dhagahbuur 82
Dhanaane 19
Dharbash 25

Dharoor 11, 40
Dharoor Valley 11, 40
Diego Garcia 76, 77
Digil 2, 3, 48, 111
Dir 2, 16, 95, 96, 111
Dire Dawa 31, 82, 89, 94
District Council 117
Djibouti xi, xii, 1, 14, 53, 54, 59, 66, 89, 101, 106, 107, 128, 129
Duduble 96
Dulmadoobe 26
Duruqbo 2
East Africa 8, 12, 13, 15, 20, 21, 31, 138
EC 106
EDU xiii, 81
Eegi 30
Eeragoo 26
Egypt 12, 75, 99, 106
El-Buur 37-39
El-Dheere 37, 38
Emil Kirsch 31
Emir Abdullahi 13
ENC 79
EPLP 88
EPRP xiii, 81
Eritrea 15, 16, 28, 34, 38, 40, 44, 45, 77, 88
Eritrean People's Liberation Front 88
Ernest Bevin 44
Ethiopia xi-xiii, 1, 2, 11, 13, 29, 33, 40, 43-46, 50-53, 59-61, 64, 65, 76, 77, 81-83, 85, 88-90, 92, 94, 106, 111, 129
F.L. James 11 Falaad 30

Fardhidin 26
Ferfeer 2
Filonardi 16, 17
Filonardi Company 16
France xii, 11, 14, 33, 43-45, 48, 52, 54, 55, 59, 65, 66, 75, 106, 131, 132
Gaameedle 2
Gadabuursi 90, 95, 96
Galgale 9
Galkayo 37, 86, 97, 10
Gambarrey 8
Garaad 4, 25-27, 37, 53, 75, 94
Garaad Makhtal 53
Garisa 55
Garowe 86
Gaullists 53
Gedo 100, 104, 108, 113
Geel-dogob 86, 88
Geledi 11, 16
General Swaine 34
George Bush 116
Georges Révoil 11
Germany 11, 12, 15, 33, 75, 103, 106
Ghalauko 14
Gheri 90
Gibil-ad 2, 108
Goday 82
Godka 101
Gola-weyne 25
Golaha Ummadda 88
Greater Somali League 49
Gudmane 2
Gumburo 26, 28
Guulwadayaal 73

Guulwade 71
Haafuun 39, 40
Haatim 2
Habar Yonis 23, 74, 96, 109
Haji Mahamed 49
Hangash 72
Hantiwadaag 71
Harar 2, 12-14, 21
Hararghe 2
Hargeysa 64, 83, 87, 89, 90, 93
Hargeysa Group 87
Harti 75, 102, 111-113, 121
Hashi Weheliye 98
Hassan Guled 54, 89
Hawaadle 96
Hawd 30, 44, 45, 47, 50, 51, 60, 61, 90
Hawiye 2, 74, 93, 94, 96-99, 101-103, 105, 107, 120, 121
Heligoland 12
Hersi Boqor 40
Hobyo 6, 15, 28-30, 33, 34, 37-39
Horn of Africa xii, xiii, 1, 3, 14, 44, 52, 54, 59, 69, 76, 98, 101, 109, 110, 115
HSDM 48
Hurdia 40, 41
IGADD 89, 106
Igal 51, 65, 66, 68, 106, 110
Ilig 18, 27-29, 31
Ilig Treaty 18, 27, 28, 31
Imam Ahmed 20
Imperial British East Africa 13
Irir 93
Isaaq 2, 32, 74, 87, 89-91, 93, 95, 96, 105-107, 109, 111, 121

Iskushuban 30, 40, 75, 86
Islaan 4
Islam 13, 20-22, 29, 31, 43, 46, 48, 110
Islam Unity 110
Issa 1, 2, 54, 92, 96, 123, 131, 132, 134
Italy 11, 13-16, 18, 19, 28, 33-38, 40, 43, 44, 46-50, 61, 75, 99, 103, 106, 119, 134
Ittixaad Al-Islaami 110
jaalle 69
Jama Ali Jama 85
Jamaame 16
Jarriban 86
Jawaya 2
Jees 93, 102, 113, 117
Jerriiban 37
Jidbaale 26, 2
Jidwaaq 90, 93
Jigjiga 2, 52, 82, 84
Jilib 104
John Speke 11
Jonathan Howe 118
Jubba 2, 12, 46, 60, 79, 85, 95, 102, 111-113
Jula 2
Kacaanka Barakaysan 75
KADU 56
Kaffa 43
Kagnew 77
KANU 56
Karen 88
Kenya xi, xii, 1, 55-57, 59, 60, 65, 76, 77, 81, 106, 111, 113, 129

INDEX

Kenya African Democratic Union 56
Khandala 86
Khartoum 21
Khedive 12
King of Shoa 13
Kismaayo 12, 60, 76, 85, 102, 104, 111-113, 121
Kissinger 77
Koofiyad Cas 86
Koofiyad Guduud 86
Laanta Buur 85
Labaatan Jirow 85
Lafaha Ragga 112
Lafoole 18
Lamu 1
Las Anod 27, 67
Las Qorey 11
Law No.1 72
Libya 44, 89, 103, 106
Splendorelli 38
London 23, 24, 29, 30, 56, 69, 72, 86, 87, 99, 111, 112
Luuq 2, 101
maalmo inkaaran 86
Magertenia 104
Mahamed Abshir xiii, 68, 110, 119
Mahamed Adan 71
Mahamed Ali 83, 92, 107
Mahamed Farah Aydiid 103, 130
Mahamed Kahin 109
Mahamed Said 97, 113
Mahamed Sheikh Osman 84, 101
Mahamed Sheikh Osman 84
Mahamed Subeer 111, 112, 121
Mahamed Warsame "Hadraawi" 73

Mahamed Yusuf 71
Mahamud Ghelle 72
Mahdist 12, 20
Majeerteen 15, 27, 29, 30, 33-35, 37, 39-41, 69, 74, 75, 84-87, 93, 96, 102, 112, 121
Majeerteen Sultanate 15, 27, 33, 34, 37, 39
Malaaq 4
Mandhera 87
Manifesto Group 98, 101
Mareehaan 74, 75, 91, 93, 96, 97, 112, 114
Marka 6, 2, 16-19, 28, 64, 85, 112
Maslah Mahamed 97
Mecca 21, 22
Menelik 13, 14, 52
Middle East 50, 75
Midgaan 2
Miinanle 25
Mike Whitlam 115
Mirashi 32
Mirreh 66, 125, 127
Morgan 97, 113
Moscow 77
Moyaale 19
Moyale 55
Mudug 30, 34, 85, 86, 104, 105, 11 121, 134
Mullah 20, 22, 23, 29, 132
Muqdisho 2, 16, 18, 19, 21, 38, 40, 41, 44, 47, 48, 51, 54, 64, 71, 74, 76,82, 85, 91, 94, 96-101, 103-105, 107, 109, 112-115, 117, 118, 121, 130
Muse Boqor 9

Mussolini 36
Mustafa Haji Nuur 85
Nairobi xiii, 21, 73, 84, 88, 113, 119, 127, 128
National Security 70-72, 84, 87, 95, 101
NER 110
NFD 13, 55-57, 60
NFDP 55
Nigeria 106, 130
North-Eastern Region 110
Northern Frontier Democratic Party 55
NPPPP 55
NSS 71, 72, 96
NUF 51
Nugaal 11, 18, 19, 25-28, 30, 32, 34, 35, 37, 85, 86, 104, 105, 110
Nugaal Valley 18, 19, 28, 30, 32, 34
Nuur Ali Qonof 67, 84
Oakley 116
OAU 61, 62, 66, 81, 106, 129, 130
Obok 1
Oday Ali 1
Ogaden 45, 60, 62, 83, 91, 131
OIC 106
Oman 106
Omar Arte 99, 107
Omar Hassan Mahamed 85
Omar Samatar 38, 39
Orientation Centres 71, 73
Oromo 1, 52, 112
Osman Nuur 84
Osmaniya 48
Ottoman Empire 31
Pasha of Turkey 12

Pasquale Mancini 15
People's Assembly 88
Public Relation Office 71
Qaali 27
Qadiriya 21, 22, 24
Qalin-shube 2
Qardho 86
Radio Muqdisho 118
Rag-xun 25
Rahanweyn 2, 3, 48, 95, 96, 108, 109, 111
Ras Waldo Gabriel 13
Red Berets 86, 87, 96, 99
Red Sea 11, 12, 14, 21, 30, 34, 43, 59, 76
Red Star 88
Reer Barawe 2, 108
Reer Fiqi 2
Reer Hamar 2, 108
Reer Sheekh 2
Reginald Maulding 56
Regional Council 117
Rendille 1
Republic of Djibouti 1, 59
Reserved Area 45, 47, 50, 51
Riig-oomane 86
Riyadh 91
Rome 38, 94, 99
Ruugga 26
Sa'ad 96
Sab 2
Sadler 21
SAF 93
Sagaalle 9
Said Jama 87
Said Samatar 59, 74, 86

INDEX

Salaad Gabayre 74
Salahiya 21, 22, 24, 25
Saleebaan 71, 96
Samaale 2
Samatar 5, 8, 15, 21, 22, 27-29, 38, 39, 50, 52, 59-61, 67, 74, 83, 86, 89, 92, 94, 101, 103, 123
SAMO 117
Sanag 111
Saudi Arabia 22, 77, 91, 106
Sayid Mahamed 18, 20-33, 35
SDA 95, 106, 117
SDLF 72, 87
SDM 95, 106, 117
SDU 70
Seamen's Union 53
Second World War xii, 43, 44, 52, 53
Security Council 115, 116, 118
Shaanshiyo 2
Shabeelle 2, 16-19, 30, 46, 60, 79, 102, 111
Sheekh Abikar Gafle 18
Sheekhaal Gendershe 2
shifta 57
Shiidle 2
shir 3, 4, 6, 8, 123
Shoa 13
Shukureere 2
Sideedle 96
Silsilad 30
Siyaad xiii, 7, 68, 70-72, 83, 84, 87-89, 91-99, 101, 103-105, 107, 121, 124, 125, 130
SNF 104, 108, 112, 117
SNL 49, 51

SNM 87, 89-91, 93-95, 98, 105, 106, 109
SNS 49
Societá Anonima Commerciale 17
Societá Filonardi 16
Somali Action Front 93
Somali Democratic Liberation Front 72, 87
Somali National Movement 87, 95, 113
Somali Officials' Union 51
Somali Patriotic Front 93
Somali Republic xii, 56, 57, 59, 129
Somali Salvation Alliance 117
Somali Workers Party 72, 87
Somali Youth League 48, 67, 69
Somalia 6, ix-xiii, 2, 5, 11, 15, 20, 21, 23, 28-31, 33-36, 40, 41, 43, 46-50, 52, 53, 55-57, 59-67, 72-74, 76-79, 81-83, 85-91, 93-97, 101, 102, 104-113, 115-130, 142
Somaliland 6, 5, 11, 12, 14-23, 26, 27, 29-34, 36-39, 41, 44-53, 55, 56, 60, 62, 65, 81-83, 88, 90-92, 101, 105, 106, 109-111, 117, 128, 130
Somaliland Republic 109
Soomaal 2
Soviet Union 65, 76, 81, 82, 87, 103
SPM 93-95, 99, 104-106, 108, 113, 117
SRC 68, 70-72, 74
SRSP 88
SSA 117

SSDF 85, 87-89, 93-95, 105, 106, 110, 117
Sublime Porte 12
Sudan 12, 20, 21, 77, 106
Suez Canal 11
Sufi 21, 2
Sultan Madar 23
Sultan of Zanzibar 12, 13, 15, 33, 112
Sultan Yusuf Ali 15, 28, 33, 34, 37
Sultanate of Hobyo 15, 37
Supreme Court 63, 68, 85
Supreme Revolutionary Council 68, 101
SWP 72, 87
SYL 48, 49, 51
Taleh 6, 30-32, 34
Tana 1, 12, 55, 111
Tana River 1, 55, 111
Tanzania 57, 66
Territorial Assembly 54
The First Charter 68 Tom Farer 119
Transitional National Council 117
Treaty of Uccialli 14, 36
Trusteeship 44, 45, 49, 61
Tumaal 2
Turkey 12
Tuula Jalam 86
Ugaas 4
Uganda 106
Union Democaratique Somalie 53
UNITAF 117
United Nations 49, 55, 61, 79, 115, 119, 127
United Somali Congress 94
UNOSOM 115, 118-120, 128
Upper Shabeelle 2, 30
US 48, 77, 78, 90, 103, 113, 116, 117, 119
USC 94, 95, 99-108, 110, 113, 117
USSR 45, 48, 52, 78, 106
Vichy 44
Victorious Leader 71
Victorious Pioneers 73
Wa'daan 16, 18, 28, 46
Wa-mbalazi 2, 108
Wa-miini 2
Wajir 55
Wardhigley 94, 99
Warsame Ali 71
Western Somali Liberation Front 53, 82, 90
Western Somaliland 6, 11, 14, 16, 26, 32, 38, 39, 45, 47, 50-53, 56, 60, 62, 81-83, 88, 90-92, 111
Weyteen 90, 93
William Christopher 11
Workers Party 72, 87
WSLF 53, 82, 90-92
Xaraf 86
Xeerka Qoyska 95
Yemen 72, 81, 106
Yibir 2
Zambia 66
Zanzibar 12, 13, 15, 33, 112
Zeila 11
Zeyla' 30
Zoli 112